Apples of Gold- Ad

Apples of Gold

A Discipleship Manual

Apples of Gold- Adeniyi OJO

Apples of Gold

A Discipleship Manual

Adeniyi Ojo

Apples of Gold- Adeniyi OJO

Published by ADENIYI OJO®

Miketonia2001@yahoo.co.uk

Written and compiled by ADENIYI OJO

Illustrations & Edition copyright © 2023, ADENIYI OJO

The moral rights of the author and illustrator has have been asserted.

Printed in United Kingdom First Published 2023

A catalogue record for this book is available from the British Library

The subject matter and statements in this book are intended and designed to be only informational and educational, It is sold with the understanding that the author and publisher are not engaged in rendering any professional advice, and so in no way responsible or liable for any loss or damages, including but not limited to the misuse of material.

All rights reserved. No part of this publication may be reproduced, copied, distributed, stored in a retrieval system, or transmitted, in any form or by any means – graphical, electronic, mechanical, photocopying, recording or otherwise, without the prior written permission of ADENIYI OJO, or as expressly permitted by law, by licence or under terms agreed with the appropriate reprographics rights organisation. Enquiries concerning reproduction outside the scope of the above should be sent to ADENIYI OJO. Any person who does any unauthorised act in relation to this publication may be liable to criminal prosecution and civil claims for damage.

This book is sold subject to the condition that it shall not, by way of trade or otherwise, be lent, re-sold, hired out, or otherwise circulated without the publisher's prior consent in any form of binding or cover other than that in which it is published and without a similar condition including this condition being imposed on the subsequent purchaser. Contact the publisher for special discounts on bulk quantity purchases by corporations, associations and others.

Dedication

With lots of love and gratitude to my wife Toun, and children: Moyo, Ibukun, Bisola and Michael.

Contents

Chapter 1: Introduction 11

Chapter 2: New Life in Christ 12

Chapter 3: Living the New Life in Christ...................... 16

    Holiness 17

    How to Live a Holy Life. 19

Chapter 4: The Joy of Salvation 23

    The Joy of Forgiveness and Acceptance 24

    The Joy of Deliverance 25

    The Joy of Divine Peace and Joy 26

    The Joy of Divine Partnership 27

    Joy of Answered Prayers and Fellowship 28

Chapter 5: Repentance 30

    John the Baptist Preached Repentance................. 31

    Jesus Christ and the Message of Repentance 32

    The Apostles Preached the Gospel of Repentance 34

    Repentance Also Applies to Believers 35

Chapter 6: Living by Grace 37

    Does Grace Mean That Sin Does Not Matter? 38

    Grace and Works (Does our Works Matter?)........ 40

Benefits of Grace 43

Chapter 7: Faith, Foolishness and Presumption 46

    Faith 47

    Presumption 49

    Foolishness 51

Chapter 8: Prayer – Communing with God 54

    The Attitude of Prayer 55

    The Act of Praying 56

    The Role of the Holy Spirit 58

Chapter 9: Sharing Your Faith 60

    Pray 61

    Prepare 62

    Proficient (Learn) 63

    Practice 66

    Practical 67

Chapter 10: Eternal Life 69

    What is Eternal Life? 69

    The Implication of Eternal Life 70

    Application of Eternal Life 74

Chapter 11: Renewing Your Mind 80

    Constituents of the Mind 81

    How to Renew Your Mind 82

    Hindrances to Renewing Your Mind 86

    Benefits of Renewing Your Mind 88

APPENDIX I	90
ACKNOWLEDGMENTS	90
APPENDIX II	91
ABOUT AUTHOR	91
APPENDIX III	92
Brief History of Charismatic Renewal Ministries	92

Apples of Gold- Adeniyi OJO

Chapter 1: Introduction

A Word fitly spoken is like apples of gold, in settings of silver. (Proverbs 25:11). This Bible verse summaries the purpose of this book. It started out as a compilation of messages that I shared at Church, Charismatic Renewal Ministries (CRM Agape House). It then evolved into a discipleship manual. I see it as an aide memoire to help new and old believers understand the basis of the Christian faith.

Our Lord Jesus commanded the Church to raise disciples, not Church members and this book attempts to contribute towards the Great Commission. As such, this book covers expected topics like salvation, prayer, The Holy Spirit, Bible study and evangelism. But also touches others like grace, eternal life, righteousness, holiness, repentance and mind renewal.

The Word of God is inexhaustible, the more you genuinely dig into it, the more revelation you will receive. It is a gift that keeps on giving.

I am still learning and growing and I hope that this book will also help you and others to love and follow Jesus even better.

But the path of the just is like the shining sun, that shines ever brighter unto the perfect day. (Proverbs 4:18)

All Bible reference are from New King James Version, except mentioned otherwise.

Chapter 2: New Life in Christ

Life can be Ironic: when you are young, you can't wait to be older. As you get older into the late 30s, you then feel like slowing the ageing process. Hence, we hear about emotional challenges like mid-life crises etc.

In the UK, the beauty industry employs over a million people and is worth £17 billion (2017). The golden grail the beauty industry is anti-ageing cream, products and treatments. We all want to look and feel younger for longer and defer growing older for as long as possible.

While growing older is not a bad thing in itself, it reminds us that we are getting closer to death. And there is a deep desire in everyone not to age or die, but to live forever. The Bible says in Ecclesiastes 3:11 ...*God has put eternity in the hearts of every one of us.*

That is why the death of a loved one, young or old is so painful, because there is a sense of loss, something precious snatched away from you and it feels like you can never get it back. Is this it? Surely there must be more to life than this!

The good news is that we are created to live forever because we are created in God's image. No human being regardless your how you look, whether rich or poor, strong or weak, educated or not educated is of less value than another human being. You are a person of worth and value because you are created in the image of God, you are the crown jewel of God's creation!

But something happened that shattered that image of God. Sin came into the world and shattered that image. The Bible in the book of Genesis chapters 1 to 3 talks about how God created the perfect sinless world, the first human beings and how sin entered the world corrupting it and separate us from God. The core problems in the world including political crisis, wars, knife crimes, infidelity in marriages, unruly behaviours, natural disasters etc are all a result of sin corrupting and decimating the world and human beings. In Romans 3:23, the Bible says *for all have sinned and fallen short of the glory (standard) of God.* In Romans 6:23, the Bible says: *For the wages (result, the consequence) of sin is death, but the free gift of God is eternal life in Christ Jesus our Lord.*

Sin is not just the bad things we do, but it is a personal inward rebellion against God, His Love and rulership over us. We want to be our own gods, reign on the throne of our hearts, be the masters of our own destinies. Like Adam & Eve in the Bible, people have been hiding and running away from the Holy, Righteous, Loving God, trying like Adam & Eve to cover their sins, make amends for their sins.

But that is not the end of the story, God said He would make good what Satan, the arch enemy made wrong, by deceiving Adam & Eve to sin against Him. The Bible is an account of God dealing with human beings from a redemptive point of view. Some people see the Bible simply as a book of rules, and while it has rules which will help us live more fulfilled lives, it is more than that. Some people see the Bible as a book of heroes - people we should emulate and aspire to be. Like David overcoming Goliath, Moses parting the Red Sea and delivering the Israelites from the oppression & slavery of Pharaoh & Egypt. Joshua and the Israelites overcoming the fortress walls and the city of Jericho.

But there is so much more. The Bible is an account of how God dealt with Man's worst enemy- sin by sending Jesus Christ (God Himself, stripping Himself of His Godliness), living a sinless life in a sinful world, showing us how to live, love, forgive and ultimately, pay the penalty for your sins, my sins and the sin of the whole world.

In exchange, He is offering us forgiveness of our sins, mercy, peace, love and the gift of eternal life to live with Him forever. The Bible says in Romans 3:24: *being justified freely by His grace through the redemption that is in Christ Jesus.*

Assuming you need extra money, but you don't have the money in the bank. Instead, you take a priced possession maybe gold jewellery to the pawn shop in exchange for cash with the hope to buy it back in the future when you have the money. That is what Jesus did for you and me. We were lost in sin – a debt we could not repay. But Jesus paid the full price and penalty for sin, to redeem (buy us) back to God. In John 1:11-12, the Bible says: *He (Jesus) came to his own, and his own people did not receive Him. But to all who did receive him, who believed in his Name, He gave the right to become children of God.* That is the great exchange. How will you respond to the great exchange? Accept it? Deny it? Delay it? It is your choice.

If you have not done so, I now invite you to become a child of God, by submitting your heart and life to Jesus as your Lord and Saviour. Receive forgiveness of sin, His peace, unconditional love and acceptance and free gift of eternal life.

Let us pray. Heavenly Father, today I come to you as a sinner, and I cannot save myself. I believe that Jesus Christ is Lord and that

He came to earth and died for my sins. Right now, I surrender my heart and life to Jesus as my Lord and Saviour. I confess that Jesus Christ is my Lord and believe in my heart that you raised Him from the dead. I now receive forgiveness of my sins and the gift of eternal life. Thank you, Lord. Amen.

Congratulations! You are now saved and have become a child of God, a citizen of heaven, an ambassador of Christ.

Chapter 3: Living the New Life in Christ

Holiness and righteousness are sometimes used interchangeably. But they are not the same and it would be helpful to understand the difference between them.

Righteousness means the ability to stand before God without the sense of guilt or inferiority as if sin never existed. Righteousness is a status we receive when we get saved so that God sees us and relate with us the same way He related with Jesus when He was on earth.

[20] Now then, we are ambassadors for Christ, as though God were pleading through us: we implore you on Christ's behalf, be reconciled to God. [21] For He made Him who knew no sin to be sin for us, that we might become the righteousness of God in Him. (2 Corinthians 5:20-21)

For if by the one man's offense death reigned through the one, much more those who receive abundance of grace and of the gift of righteousness will reign in life through the One, Jesus Christ.) (Romans 5:17)

Holiness is the outworking of righteousness which reflects in our thoughts, words and actions.

As followers of Jesus, we need both to be balanced. Holiness without righteousness could result in legalism and condemnation. Righteousness without holiness could result in lasciviousness (sinning without restraint) and is deceptive. That is why the teaching on extreme grace is wrong. Grace is not a license to continue to live in sin. Grace empowers us to say NO to sin.

¹¹ For the grace of God has appeared that offers salvation to all people. ¹² It teaches us to say "No" to ungodliness and worldly passions, and to live self-controlled, upright and godly lives in this present age, ¹³ while we wait for the blessed hope—the appearing of the glory of our great God and Saviour, Jesus Christ, ₁₄ who gave himself for us to redeem us from all wickedness and to purify for himself a people that are his very own, eager to do what is good. (Titus 2:11-14- NIV).

The role of the grace of God in living a holy life cannot be overemphasised. A lot of Christians struggle to live holy on a consistent basis not because of lack of commitment, but due to self-reliance. They strive in their own power and self-will to live holy, that may work for some time, but it then gets tedious, and frustration will set in.

The Lord does not want us to strive and stress, but yield to His Spirit, trust in His grace, make up our minds to be governed and intentionally live by His Word. You will then see that you are accidentally living a holier life by grace, than you would ever have intentionally by works (striving only in your own effort).

Holiness
¹ Finally, then brethren, we urge and exhort in the Lord Jesus that you should abound more and more, just as you received from us how you ought to walk and to please God; ² for you know what commandments we gave you through the Lord Jesus. ³ For this is the will of God, your sanctification: that you should abstain from sexual immorality; ⁴ that each of you should know how to possess his own vessel in sanctification and honor, ⁵ not in passion of lust, like the Gentiles who do not know God; ⁶ that no one should take advantage of and defraud his brother in this matter, because the Lord is the avenger of all such, as we also forewarned you and testified. ⁷ For God did not call us to uncleanness, but in holiness. ⁸ Therefore he who rejects this does not reject man, but God, who has also given us His Holy Spirit. (1 Thessalonians 4: 1-8)

Some key points to note from the above text:

- Holiness involves living the Christian life as part of a community of believers. (1 Thess. 4:1-2).
- Holiness involves living ultimately for an audience of one. You should live to please God. (1 Thess. 4:1). Sometimes the Christian life could be lonely. Maybe you are only person saved in your family, work, college etc. Know that you are not alone, Jesus said in Matthew 28:18b "I am with you always, even to the end of the age".
- Living a holy life is God's will for us. Not only is it God's will for us, but God is also willing to help us live holy lives. 1 Thess. 4:3 & Titus 2:11-14 (NIV).

It is interesting that the Bible called out sexual immorality (1 Thess.4:3). It was big during Paul's time and it still a big deal now. The world wants to reduce, deaden our sensitivity to sin and sinfulness so it is working hard to do this. Take for example a tabloid newspaper in the UK printed pictures of topless women on page 3 daily for 44 years. This was only stopped in 2015 (after much public outcry about the sexist nature and how outdated the notion was). Sexual immorality is very prevalent is our society, in movies, books, TV, language magazines, schools etc. Even to the extent that some marriages are under strain or have been destroyed by pornography. For example, one or both partners are addicted to porn, and they desire it more than their spouses. I believe that God wants to help people today. This is not to condemn you or put you down. But to provoke a holy anger in you so that you become free. Right now, I break the power of every sinful sexual desire over you and set you free from sexual bondage in Jesus Name. Amen.

How to Live a Holy Life.

You need to develop a mindset that desires to live holy. This does not mean that you will be perfect and never sin or make a mistake. You may not be sinless, but you should sin less as you grow in your Christian walk. *13 Therefore, with minds that are alert and fully sober, set your hope on the grace to be brought to you when Jesus Christ is revealed at his coming. 14 As obedient children, do not conform to the evil desires you had when you lived in ignorance. 15 But just as he who called you is holy, so be holy in all you do; 16 for it is written: "Be holy, because I am holy. (1 Peter 1:13-16).*

Actively reject and oppose ungodliness. *Therefore, laying aside all malice, all deceit, hypocrisy, envy, and all evil speaking (1 Peter 2:1).*

The Word of God is key to living holy. You therefore need to desire, consume and immerse yourself in the Word of God. *As newborn babes, desire the pure milk of the word, that you may grow thereby (1 Peter 2:2).* Newborn babies take milk on average every hour. Could this be a pointer to how often we need to take in Word of God? A helpful tip is to download the Bible app and listen to a chapter every hour or as often as you can.

Let the word of Christ dwell in you richly in all wisdom, teaching and admonishing one another in psalms and hymns and spiritual songs, singing with grace in your hearts to the Lord. (Colossians 3:16). This means you must allow the Word of God to fill and flood your mind. Reading a paragraph in a devotional is good start, but this will not really cut the mustard. God is raising an army, not civilians for the end time harvest. A good understanding and correct application of the Word of God (also described as the sword of the Spirit in Ephesians 6:17) is crucial for every believer.

Every believer is a priest unto God. As a New Testament priest, you are to offer spiritual sacrifices (prayers, intercessions and worship) to God. *⁴ Coming to Him as to a living stone, rejected indeed by men, but chosen by God and precious, ⁵ you also, as living stones, are being built up a spiritual house, a holy priesthood, to offer up spiritual sacrifices acceptable to God through Jesus Christ. (1 Peter 2:4-5).* In the Old Covenant, the priesthood was expected to live holy, sanctified lives as a testament of their devotion to the Lord. The expectation is no less in the New Covenant.

Know who you are in Christ. Walk in the reality who you are in Christ and who Christ is in you. *But you are a chosen generation, a royal priesthood, a holy nation, His own special people, that you may proclaim the praises of Him who called you out of darkness into His marvellous light; (1 Peter 2:9)*

The Holy Spirit will help you to live holy. That seems obvious, doesn't it? A lot of believers struggle to live holy because they are striving and struggling in their own power instead of relying and depending on the Holy Spirt to help them. Trying to live a holy life without the help and input of the Holy Spirit is like trying to row upstream without a paddle. In John 14:26 Jesus said: *"But the Helper, the Holy Spirit, whom the Father will send in My name, He will teach you all things, and bring to your remembrance all things that I said to you".*

The Holy Spirit is your Helper, let Him help you. How do you let the Holy Spirit help you? By acknowledging His presence and yielding every area of your life to Him. Humble yourself and admit that He is God, and you are not. Read, study, meditate on the Word of God and ask the Holy Spirit to help you understand God's Word. The Word of God and the Holy Spirit are always in agreement. *"For there are three that bear witness in heaven: the Father, the Word, and the Holy Spirit; and these three are one". (1 John 5:7).* Being baptised and filled with the Holy Spirit will take your relationship with God to a new level. Ephesians 5:18 says:

"And do not be drunk with wine, in which is dissipation; but be filled with the Spirit".

Walk in love by loving God and loving people. *³⁴ A new commandment I give to you, that you love one another; as I have loved you, that you also love one another. ³⁵ By this all will know that you are My disciples, if you have love for one another. (John 13:34-35).* God's kind of Love (Agape in Greek) is not based on feelings, it is an intentional action to do good to people because God commands us to do so. It is not even based on whether they deserve it or not. That is powerful and sobering. *²⁰ If someone says, "I love God," and hates his brother, he is a liar; for he who does not love his brother whom he has seen, how can he love God whom he has not seen? ²¹ And this commandment we have from Him: that he who loves God must love his brother also. (1 John 4:20-21).*

Walking in love does not mean you do not correct people, or you condone sin. You should correct in love instead of being overly critical and judgemental. Galatians 6:1-3 says: *Brethren, if a man is overtaken in any trespass, you who are spiritual restore such a one in a spirit of gentleness, considering yourself lest you also be tempted. ² Bear one another's burdens, and so fulfil the law of Christ. ³ For if anyone thinks himself to be something, when he is nothing, he deceives himself.*

It is easier to live holy if you live in isolation with very little human interaction. The reality for most people is that they live in community with others. This is where the rubber meets the road. People (believers and unbelievers) will test your love walk. People will hurt your feelings and you will also hurt other's feelings. Sometimes you may be unaware of what you have done or not done and vice versa. Satan will also work through people to tempt you and try to derail your walk with the Lord. Forgiveness is therefore an important in living a holy life. In Matthew 18:21-22 the Bible provides insight into forgiveness: *Then Peter came to Him and said, "Lord, how often shall my brother sin against me, and I forgive him? Up to seven times?" Jesus said to him, "I do not say to you, up to seven times, but up to seventy times seven.* You should not keep record of how many times you forgive those who hurt you. You may not maintain the same level of relationship you had prior to the incident (depending on who they are and what they did). But you owe them in Christ to release them (emotionally and spiritually). Forgiveness also frees you heart from bitterness and stress. Someone said unforgiveness is like you drinking poison and expecting the other person to get hurt. Ouch.

Prayers and Reflections

1. Read 1 Corinthians 5:21. What does it mean to be the righteousness of God in Christ and how does this impact your daily walk with the Lord?

2. Read Proverbs 7:10 and 1 Timothy 2:9. Does the way we dress matter?

3. Which area(s) in your life do you need to turn over to the Lord to live a holier life?

Chapter 4: The Joy of Salvation

Salvation through faith in Christ is big, in fact, it the biggest and the best thing that can happen to anyone. Because it marks the transition of a person from the kingdom of darkness into the Kingdom of God. *¹² and giving joyful thanks to the Father, who has qualified you to share in the inheritance of his holy people in the kingdom of light. ¹³ For he has rescued us from the dominion of darkness and brought us into the kingdom of the Son he loves, ¹⁴ in whom we have redemption, the forgiveness of sins. (Colossians 1:12-14).* We should continually give thanks for our salvation. I reckon we should give joyful thanks for our salvation at least once a day. This will help to keep your heart tender towards the Lord and develop an attitude of gratitude. Not only that, but we also have all our sins forgiven. God is no longer holding your sins against you.

Jesus described being part of God's Kingdom (salvation) as treasure worth given up all for. *⁴⁴ "The kingdom of heaven is like treasure hidden in a field. When a man found it, he hid it again, and then in his joy went and sold all he had and bought that field. (Matthew 13:44).*

Moreover, God rejoices over you and I and everyone when we become saved and become followers of Jesus Christ *⁷ I tell you that in the same way there will be more rejoicing in heaven over one sinner who repents than over ninety-nine righteous persons who do not need to repent. (Luke 15:7).*

Can you picture in your mind, the God of the whole universe and angels rejoicing and dancing over you because you are now His child? This is good news, that God rejoices over you when you become saved, and He is still looking out for you. This is the case even when you don't feel super spiritual because He loves you with an everlasting love.

¹ I lift up my eyes to the mountains, where does my help come from? ² My help comes from the Lord, the Maker of heaven and earth. ³ He will not let your foot slip, he who watches over you will not slumber; ⁴ indeed, he who watches over Israel will neither slumber nor sleep. ⁵ The Lord watches over you the Lord is your shade at your right hand; ⁶ the sun will not harm you by day, nor the moon by night. ⁷ The Lord will keep you from all harm he will watch over your life; ⁸ the Lord will watch over your coming and going both now and forevermore (Psalm 121: 1-8, NIV).

We need to begin to see ourselves the way God sees us and not the way society, culture, background, upbringing or what our present or past circumstances may have been. You may be feeling "I am not worthy or as good as that other person who has it all together". Jesus has made you worthy. *²⁸ "Come to me, all you who are weary and burdened, and I will give you rest. ²⁹ Take my yoke upon you and learn from me, for I am gentle and humble in heart, and you will find rest for your souls. (Matthew 11:28-29).*

Let us explore together some additional reasons we should be excited about our salvation and rejoice over it.

The Joy of Forgiveness and Acceptance

Our sins are forgiven (past, present and future): *¹ Blessed is the one whose transgressions are forgiven, whose sins are covered. ² Blessed is the one whose sin the Lord does not count against them and in whose spirit is no deceit. (Psalm 32:1-2 NIV).* The way God deals with us is so different from how we deal with other people. When God forgives you, He does not hold your sin against you anymore. That is true freedom and completely liberating.

We are accepted and loved by God. Not because of what we have done for Him, but what He (Jesus) has done on our behalf. *¹ Behold what manner of love the Father has bestowed on us, that we should be called children of God! Therefore, the world does not know us, because it did not know Him. ² Beloved, now we are children of God; and it has not yet been revealed what we shall be, but we know that when He is revealed, we shall be like Him, for we shall see Him as He is. ³ And everyone who has this hope in Him purifies himself, just as He is pure. (1 John 3: 1-3).* The Bible says that God first loved us, and He directed His Love to us while we were still sinners (Romans 5:8). So, your salvation is all God initiated and you are the recipient of His awesome love.

The Joy of Deliverance

It might be helpful to remind ourselves of what we have been saved from to help us appreciate God better.

⁹ A third angel followed them and said in a loud voice: "If anyone worships the beast and its image and receives its mark on their forehead or on their hand, ¹⁰ they, too, will drink the wine of God's fury, which has been poured full strength into the cup of his wrath. They will be tormented with burning sulfur in the presence of the holy angels and of the Lamb. ¹¹ And the smoke of their torment will rise for ever and ever. There will be no rest day or night for those who worship the beast and its image, or for anyone who receives the mark of its name." (Revelation 13: 9-11). You have been redeemed from eternal damnation by the virtue of submitting your life to Jesus and Your Lord and Saviour. Can you imagine what hell would be like? Unending suffering without any hope of relieve or break. The Bible says that there will be "no rest day or night" for those unfortunate enough to go to hell. Deliverance from eternal damnation is worth rejoicing over time and time again.

We have access to restoration where we have faced frustration.

¹⁵ "Whereas you have been forsaken and hated, so that no one went through you, I will make you an eternal excellence, a joy of many generations. ¹⁶ You shall drink the milk of the Gentiles, and milk the breast of kings; You shall know that I, the Lord, am your Saviour and your Redeemer, the Mighty One of Jacob. ¹⁷ "Instead of bronze I will bring gold, instead of iron I will bring silver, instead of wood, bronze, and instead of stones, iron. I will also make your officers peace, and your magistrates righteousness. ¹⁸ Violence shall no longer be heard in your land, neither wasting nor destruction within your borders; But you shall call your walls Salvation, and your gates Praise. (Isaiah 60:15-18).

Prophet Isaiah made some powerful prophetic declarations about the restoration of the Nation of Israel from state of despondency and failure. Likewise, through Christ, God has promised you restoration, promotion and security. You might be thinking that there is nothing special about you. The Lord says that you are special to Him. People may have forsaken you and cast you aside, but Jesus has reached out to lift you up. Jesus said that He has come that you might have abundant life (John 10:10). You should therefore expect and embrace the abundant life that Jesus has for you.

The Joy of Divine Peace and Joy

¹ Therefore, having been justified by faith, we have peace with God through our Lord Jesus Christ, ² through whom also we have access by faith into this grace in which we stand, and rejoice in hope of the glory of God. (Romans 5:1-2)

We have the peace of God and we have peace with God. Peace is not just the absence of problems, but the presence of God that keeps you sane and calm even when there is chaos around you. There is sanity on the inside, whilst there is chaos on the outside. People can't understand how you are still able to get it all together despite the challenges life throws at you. It is because the peace of God is keeping your heart and mind. This is a supernatural peace, not tranquillity and this peace is only available to believers in Jesus Christ.

We have access to God's presence where there is joy. *You will show me the path of life; In Your presence is fullness of joy; At Your right hand are pleasures forevermore. (Ps 16:11).* The presence of God is closer than the air you breathe because he now infuses you through His Spirit. You are joined to the Lord and one with Him (1Corinthians 6:17). He is ever present and that should well up joy in you as you access His presence through praise.

Through salvation, we have direct access to the Father through Jesus Christ. You do not need an intermediary. The Bible says in Hebrews 4:16: *Let us therefore come boldly to the throne of grace, that we may obtain mercy and find grace to help in time of need.* The throne of grace in heaven is wide open to you to access unhindered, because of the grace of God freely lavished on you through Jesus Christ. God is not in heaven, waiting for you to make a mistake and strike you. Instead, He has His hands wide open to welcome you. Change the wrong perception of God! God is for you and not against you. If you have accepted Christ Jesus as Lord, God as accepted you as His own.

The Joy of Divine Partnership

Jesus gives us His authority and He has commissioned us to act on His behalf.

[1] Then He called His twelve disciples together and gave them power and authority over all demons, and to cure diseases. [2] He sent them to preach the kingdom of God and to heal the sick. (Luke 9:1-2)

[17] Then the seventy returned with joy, saying, "Lord, even the demons are subject to us in Your name." [18] And He said to them, "I saw Satan fall like lightning from heaven. [19] Behold, I give you the authority to trample on serpents and scorpions, and over all the power of the enemy, and nothing shall by any means hurt you. [20] Nevertheless do not rejoice in this, that the spirits are subject to you, but rather rejoice because your names are written in heaven." (Luke 10:17-20)

In Luke 9:1-2, Jesus commissioned His twelve disciples (the twelve Apostles) giving them power and authority over <u>all</u> demons and sicknesses and to preach the gospel. This by extension applies to every believer. Later in Luke 10, Jesus sent seventy disciples (not the twelve Apostles) to preach the gospel and heal the sick. In Luke 10:17-20 the seventy disciples report on their exploits. It leaves us with no doubt that the power of God is for every believer and not a selected few. Mark 16:17-20 also makes this point. This means that <u>every</u> believer has the authority and backing of Jesus to effectively preach the gospel and expect signs and wonders to follow them. Please do not sell yourself short or expect anything less. Jesus gives us His authority and power so that we can fulfil divine purpose. God has a purpose for your life, His authority and power are amongst the tools to fulfil it.

Joy of Answered Prayers and Fellowship

You now have access by grace to directly approach the God the Father in Jesus' Name and get your prayers answered. *23 "And in that day you will ask Me nothing. Most assuredly, I say to you, whatever you ask the Father in My Name He will give you. 24 Until now you have asked nothing in My Name. Ask, and you will receive, that your joy may be full. (John 16:24)*. Imagine you have direct access to one of the most powerful people in the world say, The President of the United States of America. Such people have an army of protocol and security guarding access to them. But because you have direct access you can cut through all that barriers and enjoy audience with the President. Now if having such access to a mere human being thrills you, then having direct, unhindered access to the God who created the President, the world and universe should leave you breathless. I don't think as believers we have grasped the importance and implication of Jesus' statement in John 16:24. But we can start to explore the depths of it.

The joy of fellowship and Christian community.

[44] Now all who believed were together, and had all things in common, [45] and sold their possessions and goods, and divided them among all, as anyone had need. [46] So continuing daily with one accord in the temple, and breaking bread from house to house, they ate their food with gladness and simplicity of heart, [47] praising God and having favor with all the people. And the Lord added to the church daily those who were being saved. (Acts 2:44-47)

Human beings are social creatures, we are created by God to exist and thrive in community. This reflects the perfect love that exists between God the Father, God the Son and God the Holy Spirit. When believers practice and live the true fellowship and Christian community as set out in scriptures, we will make a greater impact in the world. The love practiced by the first century Christians in the Book of Acts, was so palpable, that it attracted the unbelievers who wanted a taste of the divine love found only in Jesus Christ. I believe that we should not just read and talk about it, but desire to experience it as the first century believers did. We need to disentangle from the world's system of consumerism and covetousness which leads to selfishness instead of selflessness.

Prayers and Reflections

1. God is inviting you to become a child of God, to receive Jesus as Lord and Saviour, to receive forgiveness of sin, His peace, unconditional love and acceptance and free gift of Eternal life.

2. Lord, restore to me the joy of salvation: Psalm 51: 12.

3. Reach out and receive God's healing, deliverance and breakthrough. Pray using John 10:10

Chapter 5: Repentance

It seems the phrase "I am sorry" is fast disappearing from our culture. When Politicians, Celebrities, Public Officials or Clergy fall into sin or commit a misdemeanour, they don't apologise these days. Instead, we hear the phrase "I regret my actions" or something along those lines. That is a fudge, not an apology! We need to make sure that we do not fall into the same error in terms of our relationship with our family, friends, colleagues, neighbours and God.

The Bible has a lot to say about repentance. The words 'repent' and 'repentance' occur 105 times in the Bible. 45 times in the Old Testament and 60 times in the New Testament. People familiar with the Bible would have thought it should be the other way around. That repentance would be mentioned more in the Old Testament than in the New Testament. This underlines the relevance of repentance to us.

According to Matthew Henry's commentary, to repent means to: Consider your ways, change your minds because you have thought amiss, think again, and think aright. A change of mind towards God, Christ, sin, holiness, this world and the world to come.

The change in mind must produce a change of way. Those who are truly sorry for what they have done amiss will be careful (by God's grace) to do so no more.

Repentance is a necessary duty in obedience to the command of God. In Acts 17:30, the Bible says: *And the times of this ignorance God winked at; but now commandeth all men everywhere to repent.*

Repentance is not just feeling sorry for the sin, error or heartache caused. Repentance is to change your mind, not superficially, but changing your basic attitudes and lifestyles. It involves a change of masters from sin and Satan to Jesus Christ and letting the Word of God set the agenda for your life.

Repentance relates to turning away from sin and turning to God and proving one's repentance by the fruit of a changed life. The Bible says in Acts 3:19: *Repent therefore and be converted, that your sins may be blotted out, so that times of refreshing may come from the presence of the Lord.* The saving faith that God's grace makes possible in response to hearing the gospel includes repentance.

John the Baptist Preached Repentance

Repentance was preached by John the Baptist, the fore runner of Jesus Christ. He prepared the Nation of Israel for the coming of the Messiah. In Matthew 3:1-3, the Bible says: *[1] In those days John the Baptist came preaching in the wilderness of Judea, [2] and saying, "Repent, for the kingdom of heaven is at hand!" [3] For this is he who was spoken of by the prophet Isaiah, saying: "The voice of one crying in the wilderness: 'Prepare the way of the Lord; Make His paths straight.'"* John the Baptist was a firebrand preacher who said it like it was. He was not a politically correct preacher. The Nation of Israel was in spiritual stupor, they had not received any prophetic word from God in over 400 years. That was the estimated time gap between the last book of the Bible in the Old Testament (Malachi) and the birth of Jesus Christ.

John the Baptist burst into the scene and the shook the Nation of Israel from spiritual slumber with the anointed message of repentance. Beloved, the Kingdom of Heaven is at hand. In 2 Corinthians 5:15, the Bible says: *and He (Jesus) died for all, that those who live should live no longer for themselves, but for Him who died for them and rose again.* We must repent and make God's priorities, our priorities. We must stop living for ourselves and start living for the Lord. Every notable revival in recent history, starts with or includes repentance.

John the Baptist also challenged his audience to produce evidence of repentance. In Luke 3:7-8, the Bible says: *7 Then he said to the multitudes that came out to be baptized by him, "Brood of vipers! Who warned you to flee from the wrath to come? 8 Therefore bear fruits worthy of repentance, and do not begin to say to yourselves, 'We have Abraham as our father.* John's audience were trusting in their Jewish identity to secure their salvation. John debunked the idea stating that a change of heart and not their heritage was the prerequisite to their redemption. In the same way, some people may be trusting in their Christian name or heritage to earn their salvation. It did not work then; it will not work now.

This change of heart needs to produce evidence or fruits of repentance. In Luke 3:10-14, the Bible says: *10 So the people asked him, saying, "What shall we do then?"11 He answered and said to them, "He who has two tunics, let him give to him who has none; and he who has food, let him do likewise." 12 Then tax collectors also came to be baptized, and said to him, "Teacher, what shall we do?" 13 And he said to them, "Collect no more than what is appointed for you." 14 Likewise the soldiers asked him, saying, "And what shall we do?" So he said to them, "Do not intimidate anyone or accuse falsely, and be content with your wages."*

Jesus Christ and the Message of Repentance

Repentance was key to the Kingdom message Jesus Christ preached when He began His public ministry. In Mark 1:14-15, the Bible says: *14 Now after John was put in prison, Jesus came to Galilee, preaching the gospel of the kingdom of God, 15 and saying, "The time is fulfilled, and the kingdom of God is at hand. Repent, and believe in the gospel."* After John the Baptist was imprisoned, Our Lord Jesus continued the message of repentance as a precursor for receiving the Kingdom of God.

If Jesus preached repentance, we should also preach and live repentance. The Kingdom of God is serious business and must be treated as such. *17 For the kingdom of God is not eating and drinking, but righteousness and peace and joy in the Holy Spirit. 18 For he who serves Christ in these things is acceptable to God and approved by men. (Romans 14:17-18).*

In Luke 13:1-5, Our Lord Jesus confronted His audience with the message of repentance. *1 There were present at that season some who told Him about the Galileans whose blood Pilate had mingled with their sacrifices. 2 And Jesus answered and said to them, "Do you suppose that these Galileans were worse sinners than all other Galileans, because they suffered such things? 3 I tell you, no; but unless you repent you will all likewise perish. 4 Or those eighteen on whom the tower in Siloam fell and killed them, do you think that they were worse sinners than all other men who dwelt in Jerusalem? 5 I tell you, no; but unless you repent you will all likewise perish."* Some people approached Jesus and told Him about the unfortunate situation where Pilate (the Roman Governor at that time) murdered some Galileans. It was not clear what response they were expecting, but Jesus' response to them was for them to straighten out their lives through repentance. Turn whole heartedly to the Lord. Strong stuff.

Furthermore, during the ministry of Jesus on earth, He forgave sinners, but instructed them to turn over a new leaf. For example, the woman caught in adultery in John 8:1-11. The crowd, led by the religious leaders were poised to administer the death penalty by stoning her. They asked Jesus on His thoughts, to trap Him. If Jesus said "stone her" they would have questioned the genuineness of His message of mercy and love. If Jesus said "don't stone her" they would have attempted to stone Him as well as He would be condoning the sin of adultery. Jesus delivered a masterstroke in verse 7: *...He raised Himself up and said to them, "He who is without sin among you, let him throw a stone at her first.".* The crowd convicted by their own sins fled the scene in shame. *10 When Jesus had raised Himself up and saw no one but the woman, He said to her, "Woman, where are those accusers of yours? Has no one condemned you?" 11 She said, "No one, Lord." And Jesus said to her, "Neither do I condemn you; go and sin no more."* (John 8:10-11). Jesus instructed her to turn a new leaf and turn her back on the sinful lifestyle. That is repentance. Jesus is asking us to do the same.

The Apostles Preached the Gospel of Repentance
In Mark 6:7-13, Jesus called and commissioned His twelve disciples to preach. Verse 12 makes it clear that they preached that people should repent. Mark 6:12-13 says: *12 So they went out and preached that people should repent. 13 And they cast out many demons, and anointed with oil many who were sick, and healed them.*

After His resurrection, Jesus explained and expounded the scriptures to His disciples. He also instructed them to continue to preach the message of repentance. In Luke 24:46-48, the Bible says: *46 Then He said to them, "Thus it is written, and thus it was necessary for the Christ to suffer and to rise from the dead the third day, 47 and that repentance and remission of sins should be preached in His name to all nations, beginning at Jerusalem. 48 And you are witnesses of these things.*

After Jesus' ascension into Heaven, the disciples continued to preach the gospel of repentance as instructed. On the Day of Pentecost, Peter preached that powerful message and challenged the crowd to respond by repenting. *37 Now when they heard this, they were cut to the heart, and said to Peter and the rest of the apostles, "Men and brethren, what shall we do?" 38 Then Peter said to them, "Repent, and let every one of you be baptized in the name of Jesus Christ for the remission of sins; and you shall receive the gift of the Holy Spirit. 39 For the promise is to you and to your children, and to all who are afar off, as many as the Lord our God will call." (Acts 2:37-39).* So, you see that repentance is not a side show but integral to the gospel message.

Repentance Also Applies to Believers
Based on what we have discussed so far, one might think that repentance is reserved for the unsaved only. As believers, we need to repent as required. This could be on an individual or corporate basis.

Apostle Paul urged the Church in Corinth to repent from sexual immorality that was present in the congregation. In 2 Corinthains 12:21, the Bible says: *And lest, when I come again, my God will humble me among you, and that I shall bewail many which have sinned already, and have not repented of the uncleanness and fornication and lasciviousness which they have committed.* Apostle Paul was concerned that some of the Christians in the Church in Corinth have not repented of the sins they committed. Instead, they were living in wilful rebellion and bragging of their sins. Maybe you are living in wilful rebellion to God in some areas of your life. There is opportunity for forgiveness and restoration today as you repent and turn everything over to the Lord.

In Revelation 2:4-5, Our Lord Jesus reprimanded the Church in Ephesus because they abandoned their first love and asked them to repent. *Nevertheless, I have somewhat against thee, because thou hast left thy first love. Remember therefore from whence thou art fallen, and repent, and do the first works; or else I will come unto thee quickly, and will remove thy candlestick out of his place, except thou repent.*

Furthermore, in Revelation 2:12-17, Jesus acknowledged the good works of the Church in Pergamos including at least one person being killed for their faith. Jesus still called them to order and commanded them to repent from wrong teaching, sexual immorality and idolatry. *[12] And to the angel of the church in*

Pergamos write; These things saith he which hath the sharp sword with two edges; 13 I know thy works, and where thou dwellest, even where Satan's seat is: and thou holdest fast my name, and hast not denied my faith, even in those days wherein Antipas was my faithful martyr, who was slain among you, where Satan dwelleth. 14 But I have a few things against thee, because thou hast there them that hold the doctrine of Balaam, who taught Balac to cast a stumbling block before the children of Israel, to eat things sacrificed unto idols, and to commit fornication. 15 So hast thou also them that hold the doctrine of the Nicolaitanes, which thing I hate. 16 Repent; or else I will come unto thee quickly, and will fight against them with the sword of my mouth.

What do you need to repent of? Self-centredness? Selfish ambition, wilful disobedience to the Lord and His Word? Disobedience to parents, leaders and authority figures?

Are you a Christian by association and osmosis? Or are you a Christian by personal decision and conviction? Or maybe you are Christian, but you have been living for yourself, instead of surrendering all and living for Jesus and you want to repent.

As many as I love, I rebuke and chasten: be zealous therefore, and repent. (Revelation 3:19)

Prayers and Reflections

1. Are there areas in your life that you need to repent of and turn over to the Lord?

2. Read Romans 2:4. How will you apply this in your life? Are you taking the grace of God for granted?

Chapter 6: Living by Grace

Grace is God's unmerited favour to you. Grace is God's divine ability that enables you to do what you can never achieve with your human ability, intellect or power. Grace releases God's riches to us and they all come through Jesus Christ. These riches include salvation, physical, emotional, psychological healing, deliverance, intimacy with God, divine calling, peace with God and peace of God, forgiveness of sins, answers to prayers, ability to relate with God without condemnation, righteousness, eternal life, ability to participate in the divine life, citizen of heaven, children of God, ambassadors of Christ, the fruit and gifts of the Holy Spirit, experiencing God's amazing and unconditional Love etc.

Salvation is by God's grace and you putting your faith in what Jesus did for you. *"8 For by grace are ye saved through faith; and that not of yourselves: it is the gift of God. 9 Not of works, lest any man should boast". (Ephesians 2:8-9)*. Works or self-righteousness has no role in your salvation. A lot of people think they will be saved or accepted by God because of the good works that they do. The Bible clearly says that you are saved by grace through faith. There is nothing you can do for God that will so impress Him to earn your salvation. *"But we are all as an unclean thing, and all our righteousness are as filthy rags". (Isaiah 64:6)*. God's provision of salvation is all because of His benevolence and our response to God's free gift of salvation is to receive it by faith. Trusting in Jesus alone as your Lord and Saviour is the correct response to God's amazing grace that brings salvation.

Now that you have received and submitted your heart to Jesus as your Lord and Saviour, you now need to live out your new spiritual status. The way you entered the Kingdom of God is the way you need to continue to live in the Kingdom. *"As ye have received Christ Jesus the Lord, so walk ye in Him; rooted and built up in Him, and stabilised in the faith as ye have been taught, abounding therein with thanksgiving". (Colossians 2:6).* How did you receive Christ Jesus as your Lord? By putting your faith in God's amazing grace of salvation. That is also the basis for living life in God's Kingdom after salvation. It is all by grace, through faith. You are now accepted by God because you have accepted Christ. That is awesome news! God accepts you based on He has done for you through Christ and not what you do for Him. The Bible says that we have been accepted in the beloved (Ephesians 2:6).

How do you live this out daily? Does this mean that we can go on living our lives without restrain for sin because we have now accepted Christ and God has now accepted us? NO!

Does Grace Mean That Sin Does Not Matter?
[1] What shall we say then? Shall we continue to sin, that grace may abound? [2] God forbid. How shall we, that are dead to sin, live any longer therein? Romans 6:1-2. Apostle Paul addressed head on the misconception of grace being a license to live in sin in the Book of Romans. In this passage, he clearly states that living by grace is not a license to continue to live in sin. In Paul's time as in our time, people veered off course saying, "God's grace covers me, all my sins have been forgiven anyway I can live as I want". If you really understand the grace message, you will realise that grace frees you **from** sin, grace does not free you **to** sin. Grace enables you to understand that sin is no longer your master. *For sin shall not have dominion over you: for ye are not under the law, but under grace (Romans 6:14).*

[11] For the grace of God that bringeth salvation hath appeared to all men, [12] Teaching us that denying ungodliness and worldly lusts, we should live soberly, righteously, and godly, in this present world; [13] Looking for that blessed hope, and the glorious appearing of the great God and our Saviour Jesus Christ; [14] Who gave himself for us,

that he might redeem us from all iniquity, and purify unto himself a peculiar people, zealous of good works (Titus 2:11-14). Apostle Paul again addresses the essence of God's grace.

Firstly, God's grace brings salvation to everyone. But people must respond to the offer of salvation. It is freely available for all who will receive it. This also underlines the importance of sharing the good news to make people aware of God's salvation by grace through Jesus Christ. Secondly, God's grace teaches and empowers you to say 'No' to sin, lust, worldliness, and ungodliness in all its shapes and forms. Even if everyone and their dog are living in sin around you, God's grace is mightily available to help you to resist sin. *But where sin abounded, grace did much more abound (Romans 5:20).* Thirdly, God's grace helps you to live in the light of eternity. God's grace helps you to keep eternity in view, while living life here on earth. God's grace teaches you that there is more to your life, than life on here on earth. Grace helps you to live in the anticipation of the return of Jesus or you going to meet Him in heaven. Fourthly, grace helps you to be passionate for good works. Grace gives you the desire and empowers you to make a divine mark for the Kingdom of God.

Jesus Christ dealt with our sins, past present and future sins on the cross. According to Hebrews 10:12, *But this man (Jesus) after he had offered one sacrifice for sins for ever, sat down on the right hand of God.* Even though as believers God has forgiven us our past, present and future sins, sin still matters. If you deliberately live in sin, you will open the door for the enemy (Satan) to attack and torment you. Remember the three-fold agenda of Satan? To steal, kill and destroy. *The thief cometh not, but for to steal, and to kill, and to destroy: I am come that they may have life, and that they might have it more abundantly (John 10:10).* There is consequence for sin, you are giving the enemy inroad into your life to wreak havoc. If you are deliberately living in sin, you need to repent right now. Ask God to forgive you, stop sinning and close the door to the enemy. *If we confess our sins, he is faithful and just to forgive us our sins and to cleanse us from all unrighteousness (1 John 1:9).*

Grace and Works (Does our Works Matter?)
We have established that salvation is by grace through faith. It is not based on what you do for God. That is what the Bible refers to as works. Works is trying to gain God's approval based on your own performance. The harder you work, the more blessings you receive. That was the mode of operation under the old covenant. In the new covenant, we receive all God's blessings by grace. The Bible says in John 1:16-17: *And of his fullness have we all received, and grace for grace. For the law was given by Moses, but grace and truth came by Jesus Christ.*

You are not saved **by** your good works, but you are saved **to do** good works. Ephesians 2:10 says: *For we are his workmanship, created in Christ Jesus unto good works, which God hath before ordained that we should walk in them.* Through salvation, which is your union with Jesus, you are mandated to do good works that God had already prepared for you to do.

Our Lord Jesus also made the same point in Matthew 5:14-16 about His followers doing good works: *Ye are the light of the world. A city that is set on a hill cannot be hid. Neither do men light a candle, and put it under a bushel, but on a candlestick; and it giveth light unto all that are in the house. Let your light so shine before men, that they may see your good works, and glorify your Father which is in heaven.* As followers of Jesus, your good works should be visible, impactful and tangible. A lot of people have good intentions, but good intentions by themselves, are not good enough. Your good intentions must be followed through with the corresponding actions. That is what it means to be a follower of Jesus. Yes, you should pray for your community, neighbours and circles of influence. But you also need to take concrete steps to demonstrate the love of God to them.

The good works you do here on earth matter, because they will be tested by God's fire. *¹¹ For other foundation can no man lay than that is laid, which is Jesus Christ, ¹² Now if any man build upon this foundation gold, silver, precious stones, wood, hay, stubble; ¹³ Every man's work shall be made manifest: for the day shall declare it, because it shall be revealed by fire; and the fire shall try every man's work of what sort it is. (1 Corinthians 2:12-14).* The Bible is saying that your works will be tested by fire to ascertain the quality of the work you did for God while on earth. So, your good works matter, not to get saved, but in response to your salvation and desire to expand God's Kingdom. What you do for God matters, but the attitude with which you do it matters even more. *Let nothing be done through strife or vainglory; but in lowliness of mind let each esteem other better than themselves (Philippians 2:4).*

In 2 Corinthians 5:10 the Bible says: *For we must all appear before the judgement seat of Christ; that everyone may receive the things done in his body, according to that he hath done, whether it be good or bad.* Taking the two passages (1Corinthans 2:12-14 and 2 Corinthians 5:10) you will see that at the Judgement Seat of Christ, your works will be tested by fire and rewarded accordingly.

Your good works will be rewarded. In the Parable of the Talents Our Lord Jesus painted the picture of God rewarding His people for their good works. The lord (a representation of God) commended his enterprising servants with the words *"Well done, good and faithful servant; you were faithful over a few things, I will make you ruler over many things. Enter into the joy of your lord". (Matthew 25: 21 & 23).* Also, in the Book of Revelation chapters 2 and 3, our Lord Jesus encouraged and reprimanded the 7 Churches in Asia minor. He repeatedly referred to rewards awaiting the faithful believers for example, to the Church in Laodicea He said: *"To him who overcomes I will grant to sit with*

Me on My throne, as I also overcame and sat down with My Father on His throne". (Revelation 3:21).

You might now be thinking that you need to strive really hard in our own effort to do something for God. Let us learn from Apostle Paul in terms of how he approached ministry. In 1 Corinthians 15: 9-10, the Bible says: *For I (Paul) am the least of the apostles, who am not worthy to be called an apostle, because I persecuted the church of God. But by the grace of God I am what I am, and His grace toward me was not in vain; but I laboured more abundantly than they all, yet not I, but the grace of God which was with me.* Apostle Paul who wrote two thirds of the New Testament said that he laboured more than the other Apostles. His work still speaks volumes today. He did not rely on his own effort only; he leaned on the grace of God to propel him into great accomplishments. He recognised and tapped into the tremendous grace of God available to him. You and I can and should do likewise – You work and labour by grace. When you learn to lean on God's grace, burnout in ministry fizzles away.

Every good work you do for the Kingdom of God is being recorded and will be rewarded. For your works to be rewarded appropriately, it must be done according to the divine pattern and in love. In 1 Corinthians 13:1-3 the Bible says: *Though I speak with the tongues of men and of angels, but have not love, I have become sounding brass or a clanging cymbal. And though I have the gift of prophecy, and understand all mysteries and all knowledge, and though I have all faith, so that I could remove mountains, but have not love, I am nothing. And though I bestow all my goods to feed the poor, and though I give my body to be burned, but have not love, it profits me nothing.* Love for God and people must underpin everything you do in the Kingdom of God.

Benefits of Grace

We cannot exhaust the benefits of grace. They are so numerous but let us set out a few of them.

Salvation from the clutches of sin, death and Satan is so profound, that it will take eternity to unravel. For me, is the number one benefit of grace. But it gets even better, because we are no longer enemies of God, we can now have one-to-one, heart-to-heart intimate relationship with God. In Romans 5:1-2, the Bible says: *Therefore, having been justified by faith, we have peace with God through our Lord Jesus Christ, through whom also we have access by faith into this grace in which we stand, and rejoice in hope of the glory of God.*

By grace you can stand against challenges of life and come out victorious on the other side. Apostle Paul continues his discuss in Romans 5:3-5. *And not only that, but we also glory in tribulations, knowing that tribulation produces perseverance; and perseverance, character; and character, hope. Now hope does not disappoint, because the love of God has been poured out in our hearts by the Holy Spirit who was given to us.* As a result of standing in grace (Romans 5:2), you are equipped to glory in tribulations. Not glory **for** tribulations, but glory **in or during** tribulations and challenges. The grace of God infuses perseverance, godly character and hope in you.

By grace you are commissioned by God to reign in life. In Romans 5:17, the Bible says: *For if by the one man's offense death reigned through the one, much more those who receive abundance of grace and of the gift of righteousness will reign in life through the One, Jesus Christ.).* There is a divine mandate for you to dominate life and not to be dominated by life. Some other translations of the verse used the phrases "kings of life", "rule in life" and "live like kings". This resonates with the divine mandate given to man at creation. Genesis 1:28 says: *Then God blessed them, and God said to them, "Be fruitful and multiply; fill the earth and subdue it; have dominion over the fish of the sea, over the birds of the air, and over every living thing that moves on the earth."*

Grace helps you to serve God acceptably and with godly reverence. Hebrews 12: 28-29 says: *Therefore, since we are receiving a kingdom which cannot be shaken, let us have grace, by which we may serve God acceptably with reverence and godly fear. For our God is a consuming fire.* God wants His children to be free with him in terms of relating with Him. However, we must not become overfamiliar with God to the point that we do not take His instructions seriously. The Bible says that there is an acceptable way to serve God. Conversely, that means there is an unacceptable way to serve God. Grace will help you to offer acceptable and pleasing worship to God with respect and awe.

Grace helps you to grow and mature in Christ. God grace will help you to be become more like Jesus on this side of eternity – if you yield to the grace of God. 2 Peter 3:18 says: *But grow in the grace and knowledge of our Lord and Savior Jesus Christ. To Him be the glory both now and forever. Amen.* 2 Peter 1:2 also says *Grace and peace be multiplied to you in the knowledge of God and of Jesus our Lord.* This verse is saying that grace is not static and can be multiplied. That means that the grace of God at work in you and for you can increase and multiply. There is no limit to the grace of God that you operate in. Only you can limit or stifle the grace of God in your life. No wonder the Bible says, "I do not frustrate the grace of God" (Galatians 2:21a). Notice that both passages (2 Peter 1:2 and 2 Peter 3:18) mention knowledge alongside grace as the avenue to grow in grace and experience multiplication of grace. This knowledge is not head knowledge, but intimate, relationship-based knowledge. Just like you can know information about a famous person, the facts and figures. That is quite different from knowing the person on a personal basis. God want you to know and relate with Him personally. Personal relationship with God is an important aspect of growing and multiplying the grace of God in and on you.

God's grace helps you to put life's disappointments and challenges in the right perspective. That is in the light of eternity. Through grace we rejoice in the hope of the glory of God (Romans 5:2). The ultimate glory of God is being with Him for eternity. That is awesome!

Prayer and Reflections

1) What do you understand grace to be?
2) Read Galatians 2:21. What does it mean to frustrate the grace of God?
3) How are you demonstrating the love and grace of God to your circle of influence?

Chapter 7: Faith, Foolishness and Presumption

Imagine this, someone needs to see a doctor, but he or she would not mind being seen by a person who did not complete medical school! Or having your boiler, central heating or car repaired by someone who failed the qualifying exams. I am sure no one would want that. We want to ensure that people who deal with us are professional, capable and qualified. In order words, people who know what they are doing.

The Christian life is like that: God wants us to be capable believers: strong in the Word, filled and led by the Holy Spirit, have godly character, experience and demonstrate God's Love to all around us. *14that we should no longer be children, tossed to and fro and carried about with every wind of doctrine, by the trickery of men, in the cunning craftiness of deceitful plotting, 15 but, speaking the truth in love, may grow up in all things into Him who is the head—Christ: (Ephesians 4:14 -15)*

At this point, let us define the three keywords in this chapter: faith, presumption, and foolishness to help us as we go along.

Faith is trust, reliance or confidence in God, His ability, and the integrity of His Word. Faith is also acting on the Word of God.

Presumption is to think or assume that something is true, but without proof or supporting evidence to back it up.

Foolishness is lacking good sense or judgement, being silly or unwise.

Faith

Faith is trust, reliance or confidence in God, His ability and the integrity of His Word. Faith involves, putting your trust in, hanging your hope on God and the fact that His Word never fails.

[89] Forever, O Lord, Your word is settled in heaven. [90] Your faithfulness endures to all generations; You established the earth, and it abides. (Psalm 119: 89-90)

Faith involves more than a belief in God, His ability, and the integrity of His Word. Faith also requires positive action, waiting on God and being persistent in standing on God's promises even when 'evidence' shows otherwise.

[8] By faith Abraham obeyed when he was called to go out to the place which he would receive as an inheritance. <u>And he went out</u>, not knowing where he was going. [9] By faith he dwelt in the land of promise as in a foreign country, dwelling in tents with Isaac and Jacob, the heirs with him of the same promise; [10] for he waited for the city which has foundations, whose builder and maker is God. (Hebrews 11: 8-10)

James, the stepbrother of Jesus helps to press home this point further. *[18] But someone will say, "You have faith, and I have works." Show me your faith without your works, and I will show you my faith by my works. [19] You believe that there is one God. You do well. Even the demons believe—and tremble! [20] But do you want to know, O foolish man, that faith without works is dead? [21] Was not Abraham our father justified by works when he offered Isaac his son on the altar? [22] Do you see that faith was working together with his works, and by works faith was made perfect? [23] And the Scripture was fulfilled which says, "Abraham believed God, and it was accounted to him for righteousness." And he was called the friend of God. [24] You see then that a man is justified by works, and not by faith only. [25] Likewise, was not Rahab the harlot also justified by works when she received the messengers and sent them out another way? ²⁶ For as the body without the spirit is dead, so faith without works is dead also. (James 2:18-26)*

So beloved, obedience or positive action is the proof of faith. Not just accepting or mentally agreeing that the Word of God is true. Positive action could be any or a combination of walk the talk; confessing God's Word, ensuring that our conversations are filled with faith words and praising God.

Praising God is a vital sign of walking the in faith. God confirmed this about Abraham, the father of faith. *²⁰ He (Abraham) did not waver at the promise of God through unbelief, but was strengthened in faith, <u>giving glory to God</u>, ²¹ and being fully convinced that what He had promised He was also able to perform. ²² And therefore "it was accounted to him for righteousness." (Romans 4:20-22)*. You and I can praise God even when we do not feel like doing so. Praising and worshipping God should not be based on feelings, but an intentional decision to give glory to God because He is good, for His mercies, His salvation and Eternal Life He has given us in Christ Jesus. We need to develop an attitude of gratitude.

The Word of God is the source of faith, our faith like muscles grow with usage. Start using your faith where you are, based on what you know from God's Word. Use your faith in small matters for example against headaches, etc, offer to pray for others to be healed. *¹⁶ For I am not ashamed of the gospel of Christ, for it is the power of God to salvation for everyone who believes, for the Jew first and also for the Greek. ¹⁷ For in it the righteousness of God is revealed from faith to faith; as it is written, "The just shall live by faith." (Romans 1:16-17)*

Presumption

Presumption is to think or assume that something is true, but without proof or supporting evidence to back it up. Do you remember the illustration at the introduction of the quack doctor or the wanna be engineer or mechanic? They are presumptuous in that they have some information about the professions but lack evidence in the form of qualification or track record to back up their claims. They are dangerous both to themselves and others. Partial information and arrogance are deadly combination.

In our walk with God, God wants us to have a first-hand knowledge better put, inspiration from Him. *12 For this reason I also suffer these things; nevertheless, I am not ashamed, <u>for I know whom I have believed and am persuaded</u> that He is able to keep what I have committed to Him until that Day. (2Timothy 1:12).* For one to be fully persuaded like Paul, he or she needs to mediate on the Word of God to the point that the Word becomes God speaking to you personally. The Word of God is not just a good idea, something nice or motivational message you heard in Church or preached by your favourite preacher.

We also need to act on the Word of God in line with our belief. If your actions do not align with your belief, you merely agree that the Word of God is true, you do not really believe it. Our actions confirm or contradict our belief.

Let us consider a case in the Bible of people acting presumptuously.

11 Now God worked unusual miracles by the hands of Paul, 12 so that even handkerchiefs or aprons were brought from his body to the sick, and the diseases left them and the evil spirits went out of them. 13 Then some of the itinerant Jewish exorcists took it upon themselves to call the name of the Lord Jesus over those who had evil spirits, saying, "We exorcise you by the Jesus whom Paul preaches." 14 Also there were seven sons of Sceva, a Jewish chief priest, who did so. ⁱ⁵ And the evil spirit answered and said, "Jesus I know, and Paul I know; but who are you?"

¹⁶ Then the man in whom the evil spirit was leaped on them, overpowered them, and prevailed against them, so that they fled out of that house naked and wounded. ¹⁷ This became known both to all Jews and Greeks dwelling in Ephesus; and fear fell on them all, and the name of the Lord Jesus was magnified. ¹⁸ And many who had believed came confessing and telling their deeds. ¹⁹ Also, many of those who had practiced magic brought their books together and burned them in the sight of all. And they counted up the value of them, and it totalled fifty thousand pieces of silver. ²⁰ So the word of the Lord grew mightily and prevailed. (Acts 20:11-20)

Points to note about the sons of Sceva.

- They were not believers in Jesus. Verse 13 notes that they were Jewish exorcists, and they did not have a personal relationship with Jesus.

- They thought or assumed that they could use the Name of Jesus without evidence to back it up because they were exorcists. How wrong they were!

- The result was catastrophic.

Healing is a topic, if not handled carefully could lead to people acting presumptuously. For example, you listen to or read about the experience of someone living a life free of sickness or who overcame sickness or health challenges by trusting on God's Word for healing. This in many cases could lead to the person not taking medication.

Now, not taking medication by itself is not acting in faith. Faith is based on the Word of God and trusting on the integrity of God and His Word. A personal conviction of the finished work of Jesus on cross dealing decisively with sin and sickness could then lead someone not to resort to taking medication.

People have hurt themselves or even died prematurely because they refused medical help thinking they were walking in faith. As mentioned, walking in faith in healing and all areas is based on believing and acting on the Word of God. One must be personally and fully persuaded and not 'faking to make it' or living to people's expectation. If you are not fully persuaded in terms of a health challenge, please seek the best medial help you can get. God best for us is divine health and healing but seeking medical advice or help is not a sin. In addition, you can also reach out to other believers who are more advanced in the faith journey to minister to you. In James 5:14 -15, the Bible says: *[14] Is anyone among you sick? Let him call for the elders of the church, and let them pray over him, anointing him with oil in the name of the Lord. [15] And the prayer of faith will save the sick, and the Lord will raise him up. And if he has committed sins, he will be forgiven.*

Foolishness

Foolishness is lacking good sense or judgement, being silly or unwise. We see an account in the Bible of Dinah, the daughter of Jacob, The Patriarch, acting foolishly.

[1] Now Dinah the daughter of Leah, whom she had borne to Jacob, went out to see the daughters of the land. [2] And when Shechem the son of Hamor the Hivite, prince of the country, saw her, he took her and lay with her, and violated her. [3] His soul was strongly attracted to Dinah the daughter of Jacob, and he loved the young woman and spoke kindly to the young woman. [4] So Shechem spoke to his father Hamor, saying, "Get me this young woman as a wife." [5] And Jacob heard that he had defiled Dinah his daughter. Now his sons were with his livestock in the field; so Jacob held his peace until they came. (Genesis 34:1-5)

Jacob and his family moved into a new location (Shechem) which they knew no one or what sort of people lived there. Dinah then decided to go out unaccompanied to see the daughters of the land. She went to explore a new area and neighbours without informing her parents or relations. She was exposed, unprotected, and sexually assaulted by the prince of Shechem. Perhaps, this unfortunate incident might have been prevented if she acted with better sense of judgement.

28 For which of you, intending to build a tower, does not sit down first and count the cost, whether he has enough to finish it— 29 lest, after he has laid the foundation, and is not able to finish, all who see it begin to mock him, 30 saying, 'This man began to build and was not able to finish'? 31 Or what king, going to make war against another king, does not sit down first and consider whether he is able with ten thousand to meet him who comes against him with twenty thousand? 32 Or else, while the other is still a great way off, he sends a delegation and asks conditions of peace. 33 So likewise, whoever of you does not forsake all that he has cannot be My disciple. (Luke 14:28-33)

It is foolish, not to work hard, but expect to get good grades or get promoted at work, expect your business to thrive. The diligent will become rich. (Prov. 10:4).

It is foolish to wish to have a job, but do not complete application forms, register with agencies, go to recruitment shows, do the leg work required and expect the job to fall on your laps. You think praying alone will do it or praying and confessing the Word but no corresponding action. Remember, *For as the body without the spirit is dead, so faith without works is dead also. (James 2:26).*

The flip side is also applicable for a believer. It is foolish to only depend on your ability and ignore or play down the power of God in your life. This will result in frustration.: *5 Thus says the Lord: "Cursed is the man who trusts in man and makes flesh his strength,*

Whose heart departs from the Lord. ⁶ For he shall be like a shrub in the desert, and shall not see when good comes, but shall inhabit the parched places in the wilderness, In a salt land which is not inhabited. ⁷ "Blessed is the man who trusts in the Lord, and whose hope is the Lord. ⁸ For he shall be like a tree planted by the waters, which spreads out its roots by the river, And will not fear when heat comes; But its leaf will be green, And will not be anxious in the year of drought, Nor will cease from yielding fruit. (Jeremiah 17:5-8)

God wants us to be balanced- we need pray and trust God like only that will help us and we need to work hard, grow and improve ourselves like only that will help. Like two wings to help birds fly. Both will produce bounty harvest in our lives.

In conclusion, faith is based on absolute trust in God, the integrity of His Word and taking appropriate action required.

Reflections and Prayer points

1. Pray against manifestation of foolishness in your life.

2. Pray against presumptuous living.

3. Thank God for Bible based victorious faith in your life.

Chapter 8: Prayer – Communing with God

Praying is communing with God. That implies that it is a two-way communication or dialogue. Unfortunately, for many believers, prayer is an opportunity for people to dump their needs or requests on God and end the prayer with the words in Jesus Name. Whilst the Lord wants us to make our requests to Him through prayer, requests or petitions should really form a small aspect of our prayer life. Approaching prayer in this way, makes it a monologue, dull and full of repetition. The Lord Jesus warns us against using vain repetitions in our prayers.

There are different types of prayers. These include intercessory, petition, warfare, worship, and mediation. We will be looking into what is using the 'model prayer' the Lord's prayer as a guide.

[5] "And when you pray, you shall not be like the hypocrites. For they love to pray standing in the synagogues and on the corners of the streets, that they may be seen by men. Assuredly, I say to you, they have their reward. [6] But you, when you pray, go into your room, and when you have shut your door, pray to your Father who is in the secret place; and your Father who sees in secret will reward you openly. [7] And when you pray, do not use vain repetitions as the heathen do. For they think that they will be heard for their many words. [8] "Therefore do not be like them. For your Father knows the things you have need of before you ask Him. [9] In this manner, therefore, pray: Our Father in heaven, Hallowed be Your name. [10] Your kingdom come. Your will be done on earth as it is in heaven. [11] Give us this day our daily bread. [12] And forgive us our debts, as we forgive our debtors. [13] And do not lead us into temptation but deliver us from the evil one. For Yours is the kingdom and the power and the glory forever. Amen. [14] "For if you forgive men their trespasses, your heavenly Father will also forgive you. [15] But if you

do not forgive men their trespasses, neither will your Father forgive your trespasses. (Matthew 6: 5-15)

The Attitude of Prayer

Hypocrites love to pray (verse 5). They love to use prayer as a measure of how spiritual they are or impress people. Do not use prayer to show how spiritual you are. You are not trying to impress people. You are not even trying to impress God. God sees through all the smokes and mirrors. Get real in your attitude and in the words, you use in prayer. Remember you are praying to your Heavenly Father.

Shut out distractions (verse 6). We live in 24-7 age where information and content are being created every second. In some cases, people are being addicted to their phone or electronic devices. Switch off the TV, your phone, tablet, laptop and social media! It is very helpful if you can get quiet place or time to pray. For example, early in the morning- depending on your personal schedule. This will help you to be laser focussed.

Don't try and impress God by using 'spiritual words' that you do not really mean or understand. Neither use vain repetitions like "O God do it, Oh God do it, I say oh God do it"! God is not deaf. He is willing and able to help you. God is not your problem. The Bible says that that our ever-present help in times of need.

The Lord is more interested in the disposition of your heart, than the display of your words. Be honest, authentic, and sincere in your heart. That is what translates into a heartfelt, powerful prayer as mentioned in James 5:16-18 . *[16]Therefore confess your sins to each other and pray for each other so that you may be healed. The prayer of a righteous person is powerful and effective. [17] Elijah was a human being, even as we are. He prayed earnestly that it would not rain, and it did not rain on the land for three and a half years. [18] Again he prayed, and the heavens gave rain, and the earth produced its crops.*

Effective and effectual prayer is not mouthing the 'right' words, but an alignment between the mouth and heart based on the Word of God.

The Act of Praying
The foundation of true praying is based on relationship with God as our Heavenly Father. In Matthew 6:9, Jesus started the model prayer with the words 'Our Father'. What sweet fellowship those words ensued. Do you see God as your Father, not just God in heaven?

Revere, honour, adore God as Holy, Righteous and Perfect (Matthew 6:9b). His Name is Holy, He is Holy, everything about Him is Holy. There is no unrighteousness in Him. *Every good and perfect gift is from above, coming down from the Father of the heavenly lights, who does not change like shifting shadows. (James 1:17).*

Use songs of worship to adore Him. *⁴ Enter his gates with thanksgiving and his courts with praise; give thanks to him and praise his name. ⁵ For the Lord is good and his love endures forever; his faithfulness continues through all generations (Psalms 100:4-5)*

Don't come into prayer with gripping and complaining. We are challenged to come into His presence with praise. One translation of that verse says the password is praise. I love it. Remember the Lord already knows your problems even before you pray about them. So, learn to relax in His presence. This is simple to say, it may not be that easy to do. But we need to train our minds to live by the Word and not by what we think or feel.

Surrender yourself, your plans to Him. Submit to His sovereignty over your life, family, work, community, circle of influence and Country. (Matt.6:10). God's plans for us are far bigger, far better more beautiful than any one we can come up. Surrendering to the Lord will not take the fun out of our life. On the contrary, it will add colour, purpose, and fulfilment far beyond your wildest dreams.

Matthew 6:11 encourages us to make our requests known to the Lord. What do you pray about? You can pray for your personal needs, family needs, work or business, work colleagues, neighbours, your circle of influence, your Church, Church family, your Community, your Country and world events. The Bible commands us to pray for our leaders and people in authority.

[1] I urge, then, <u>first of all</u>, that petitions, prayers, intercession and thanksgiving be made for all people. [2] for kings and all those in authority, that we may live peaceful and quiet lives in all godliness and holiness. [3] This is good, and pleases God our Savior, [4] who wants all people to be saved and to come to a knowledge of the truth.

Asking God for forgiveness and forgiving others who hurt us is an important aspect of prayer. We confess our sins to the Lord, in an open, honest way, receiving His forgiveness and mercy (Matthew 6:12). We must refuse the enemy's lies about whether God has really forgiven you. But we also use this time to forgive, release people who have hurt us (Matthew 18:21-22). *Then Peter came up and said to him, "Lord, how often will my brother sin against me, and I forgive him? As many as seven times?" Jesus said to him, "I do not say to you seven times, but seventy-seven times.* Forgiveness does not mean we leave ourselves open for people to hurt us repeatedly, depending on the circumstances, but we must release them from the past. It is also for our own good and making sure we don't miss heaven. Someone said that unforgiveness is like you taking poison and expecting the other person to get hurt. Unforgiveness will hurt you long after the person or people who hurt you have moved on.

I fully understand that this is simple to say, but not easy to do. However, the Lord will never ask us to do things He has not given us the grace to do. Make a quality decision to forgive, then look for ways to be a blessing to them. This helps to break the power of bitterness over you and let the love of God flow through you.

In Matthew 6:13a, The Lord Jesus points out that we should ask God for protection, security, strength and wisdom to overcome temptation and evil people. He promised to give us protection. *The angel of the Lord encamps around those who fear him, and he delivers them. (Psalm 34:7)*

In Matthew 6:13b, we are encouraged to declare our victory over sin, sickness, all the works of the devil. *The reason the Son of God appeared was to destroy the works of the devil (1John 3:8b).* We proclaim and stand on the victory of the cross that Jesus purchased for us. *⁴ for everyone born of God overcomes the world. This is the victory that has overcome the world, even our faith. ⁵ Who is it that overcomes the world? Only the one who believes that Jesus is the Son of God. (1 John 5:4-5).* We need to proactively resist the devil and he will flee from us. *Submit yourselves, then, to God. Resist the devil, and he will flee from you. (James 4:7)*

The Role of the Holy Spirit

The role of the Holy Spirit in empowering us and in the place of prayers cannot be over emphasised. *Likewise, the Spirit helps us in our weakness. For we do not know what to pray for as we ought, but the Spirit himself intercedes for us with groanings too deep for words. And he who searches hearts knows what is the mind of the Spirit, because the Spirit intercedes for the saints according to the will of God. (Romans 8:26-27)*

Have you ever wanted to pray, but you were short of words? Or you felt a need to pray for someone who just popped into your mind? But you really did not know what to pray about. With your limited understanding, you may have prayed a generic prayer for them. However, when you pray in tongues you pray the mind of God about the person or the issue at hand. When we pray according to His will, He hears us.

I recall years back; my Dad went to pick up Mum from the airport. I had a leading not to accompany him. Whilst I was a home, I was praying, then the picture of my Mum flashed across my mind. I felt the urge to pray in tongues more intensely for her. After a few minutes I had a relief on the inside of me. When she arrived home, she narrated the incident at the airport. As she was chatting with my Dad, a pickpocket stole her purse. She immediately felt or noticed that something was wrong and raised an alarm, they chased the thief and after some 50m, he dropped the purse, and it was retrieved. The incident happened while I felt the urge to pray in tongues for her.

To turbo charge your walk with God and prayer life, you really need to be filled with the Holy Spirit and take advantage of the heavenly prayer language of speaking in tongues. *[38] And Peter said to them, "Repent and be baptized every one of you in the name of Jesus Christ for the forgiveness of your sins, and you will receive the gift of the Holy Spirit. [39] For the promise is for you and for your children and for all who are far off, everyone whom the Lord our God calls to himself. (Acts 2:38-39).*

Chapter 9: Sharing Your Faith

Sharing your faith is one of the spiritual disciplines we need to do to be spiritually alert and fresh. I believe that a lot of believers are missing out and not enjoying the Christian life to its fullness if they are not regularly involved in evangelism and sharing their faith.

It is heartbeat of the Father and number one priority of the Kingdom. This why Jesus came to reconcile men back to God.

15 And He said to them, "Go into all the world and preach the gospel to every creature. 16 He who believes and is baptized will be saved; but he who does not believe will be condemned. 17 And these signs will follow those who believe: In My name they will cast out demons; they will speak with new tongues; 18 they will take up serpents; and if they drink anything deadly, it will by no means hurt them; they will lay hands on the sick, and they will recover." 19 So then, after the Lord had spoken to them, He was received up into heaven, and sat down at the right hand of God. 20 And they went out and preached everywhere, the Lord working with them and confirming the word through the accompanying signs. Amen.

Our Lord Jesus went further in the Gospel in Matthew where he commanded His followers to raise disciples.

16 Then the eleven disciples went away into Galilee, to the mountain which Jesus had appointed for them. 17 When they saw Him, they worshiped Him; but some doubted. 18 And Jesus came and spoke to them, saying, "All authority has been given to Me in heaven and on earth. 19 Go therefore and make disciples of all the nations, baptizing them in the name of the Father and of the Son and of the Holy Spirit, 20 teaching them to observe all things that I have commanded you; and lo, I am with you always, even to the end of the age." Amen

Let us look into five aspects instrumental to effectiveness in sharing your faith with others. These are Pray, Prepare, Practice, Proficient (Learn) and Practical.

Pray

We need to pray for ourselves to have a heart for our unsaved family members, friends, colleagues and neighbours. If we don't have genuine compassion for the lost, all we do will be mechanical and lifeless. *But when He (Jesus) saw the multitudes, He was moved with compassion for them, because they were weary and scattered, like sheep having no shepherd. (Matthew 9:36).*

Are you moved with compassion for the lost? I mean really moved with compassion for the lost? What is your attitude towards your unsaved colleagues, neighbours, family and friends? We need to pray for genuine compassion for the lost because they are risk of a Christless eternity.

We need to pray that the Lord will open the hearts of the lost and we need to break the power of the enemy over their lives. *³ But even if our gospel is veiled, it is veiled to those who are perishing, ⁴ whose minds the god of this age has blinded, who do not believe, lest the light of the gospel of the glory of Christ, who is the image of God, should shine on them. (2Corinthians 4:3-4)*

We need to pray for opportunities to preach the gospel and share Jesus in our everyday lives. Oftentimes, Christians limit sharing their faith to a 'special' event such as evangelism organised by the Church, inviting people to Church or special events. We should actively, look for, pray for, opportunities to share our faith with others in our circle of influence. *⁷Ask, and it will be given to you; seek, and you will find; knock, and it will be opened to you. ⁸ For everyone who asks receives, and he who seeks finds, and to him who knocks it will be opened. (Matthew 7:7-8)*

Prepare
Being prepared to share your faith will involve looking for and identifying touchpoints in your community, circle of influence to share the gospel. For example, bus stops, train stations, shopping malls, high streets, cinemas, car boot sales, celebrations like your birthdays or events such as Easter, Christmas, Bank holidays and community events. *But sanctify the Lord God in your hearts, and always be ready to give a defense to everyone who asks you a reason for the hope that is in you, with meekness and fear (1 Peter 3:15)*

Intentionally, deliberately, purposefully make friends and contacts for the sake of the gospel. For example, join your local gym, mothers and toddlers' group, running club, attend councillors' meetings, join community social media groups, the possibilities are limitless. You need to move out of your comfort zone. How many non-Christian friends and contacts do you have?

[19] For though I am free from all men, I have made myself a servant to all, that I might win the more; [20] and to the Jews I became as a Jew, that I might win Jews; to those who are under the law, as under the law, that I might win those who are under the law; [21] to those who are without law, as without law (not being without law toward God, but under law toward Christ), that I might win those who are without law; [22] to the weak I became as weak, that I might win the weak. I have become all things to all men, that I might by all means save some. [23] Now this I do for the gospel's sake, that I may be partaker of it with you. (1 Corinthians 9:19-23)

I hope you know that this does not mean living a sinful lifestyle to win the lost. We are in the world, but not of the world. Our Lord Jesus set the example for us. He was in the world, impacted the world and but He was not tainted by the world's culture, system or value. He has empowered you by the Holy Spirit to do likewise.

It is also useful to have a variety of Christian literature: tracts, flyers, mini books at hand to share. You can buy from Christian stores, create yours and or use the ones provided by your local Church.

Look for practical ways to be a blessing to your community. People don't care how much you know, until they know how much you care. For example, can you offer to trim your neighbour's overgrown hedges, mow their lawn, provide school supplies for needy families, offer to pray for people at community events, volunteer with your local foodbank? The possibilities are endless, and you need to use your imagination. Yes, it will require you to put yourself out there. But that is part of the being a disciple of Jesus. It involves knowing Him and making Him known.

Preparation also involves reading books, watching videos about how to share your faith. These could be books on apologetics, one-to-one conversations, how to effectively share your salvation experience, one-to-many conversations. Sharing your salvation experience involves who you were before you got saved, how you got saved and the difference between what were and what you are now. No one can refute your experience. They may not agree with it. But it is what it is.

Proficient (Learn)

Learn how to develop a mindset that searches for opportunities to share the gospel. Develop a soul winner's mindset. For example, continuously affirm that there are so many souls out there waiting to hear and respond to the good news of Jesus Christ. I declare that souls are being saved, healed and delivered in Jesus' Name. It is not going to be easy especially if you are going at it alone or you do not have support network to start with. But you are never alone, are you? Jesus said …."I am with you always, even to the end of the age". (Matthew 28:20b).

Ask the Holy Spirt to help you share the gospel and develop confidence in doing so regularly. *Ask of Me, and I will give you the nations for your inheritance, and the ends of the earth for Your possession. (Psalm 2:8).*

Learn different approaches to sharing the gospel. These could include direct, cognitive, sharing your testimony, practical, power, invitational, testimonial, relational and adventurous.

Direct approach can be seen in Acts 2. On the Day of Pentecost when the Holy Spirit came on the Apostles, a crowd gathered round, and Peter preached a direct straight to the point message that required a response. The focal point of the message was Jesus is the Messiah (Saviour) that God promised Israel and by repenting and believing on Jesus, they would be saved from their sins and receive God's gift of eternal life.

The cognitive or intellectual approach involves using Biblical reasoning to address intellectual roadblock to people believing. A similar approach is used by apologetics to address barriers to belief and help them understand that the Christianity is not just 'blind faith'. Some recommended books are More than a Carpenter, and Evidence that requires a verdict by Josh McDowell. Another one is The Case for Christ by Lee Strobel. It is about a journalist's personal investigation into the evidence for Jesus. In the Bible, we see in Acts 17 where Apostle Paul reasoned with philosophers and intellectuals of his time.

Sharing your personal testimony of how you came to faith is a very powerful way to evangelise. You will be surprised that people will be open to how Jesus changed you. This could be structured as who you were before you got saved, how you got saved and the difference Jesus has and is making in you since you got saved. Your testimony does not need to be dramatic or miraculous like Apostle Paul's. It could just be how God changed me from being a 'religious person' who attends Church to now having a personal, vibrant, real relationship with God through Jesus Christ.

Practical approach involves doing acts of kindness for people with the view of it opening doors to share the good news with them. It is showing God's love in practical ways. It is important that we find ways of incorporating sharing the good news into the acts of kindness. This could range from telling people your motivation for what you are doing, handing out gospel tracts or literature etc. There is a risk that people get caught up in helping people that sharing the good news is excluded. We must ensure that we keep the gospel at the heart of whatever we are doing.

Power approach involves demonstrating the miraculous power of God with a view to open doors to sharing your faith with others. You could offer to pray for people with needs (physical, emotional health challenges etc). Our Lord Jesus has empowered us to demonstrate His power in His Name. *5 These twelve Jesus sent out and commanded them, saying: "Do not go into the way of the Gentiles, and do not enter a city of the Samaritans. 6 But go rather to the lost sheep of the house of Israel. 7 And as you go, preach, saying, 'The kingdom of heaven is at hand.' 8 Heal the sick, cleanse the lepers, raise the dead, cast out demons. Freely you have received, freely give. (Matthew 10:5-8)*

Using the power of questions to share your faith. Questions was central to Jesus' ministry. He was asked 183 questions in the gospels, He directly answered 3. Jesus asked over 300 questions in the gospel. "Who do men say that I, the Son of Man, am?" (Matthew 16:13) and "But who do you say that I am?" (Matthew 16:15). You could also leverage this approach. For example, "what do you think will happen to people after death?" "How did you come to that conclusion?" Then point them to the Bible- The Word of God. Asking questions can open doors for conversations about Jesus without appearing to 'preach at them'. With the help of the Holy Spirit, the central message of the gospel is being passed across.

Practice

Take action. Taking corresponding action is very important. You can have all the information in the world, but if you do not act on it, it will remain theoretical, not practical. If you still do not act, this could lead to frustration because there is a gap between what you know and what you are experiencing.

I believe a lot of Christians are not enjoying the fulness of their salvation because they do not regularly share their faith with others. We are commanded to share the good news with others. It is the great commission, not the great suggestion. *15 And He said to them, "Go into all the world and preach the gospel to every creature. 16 He who believes and is baptized will be saved; but he who does not believe will be condemned. (Mark 16:15-16)*

I do not believe that God wants to guilt trip us into sharing our faith. He will not stop answering your prayers or loving you. But you may not experience the fulness of what God has for you. This is not God withholding from you, this is you not fully accessing all that the Lord has for you.

Keep on taking action even when you do not feel like doing it or seeing any results. *And let us not grow weary while doing good, for in due season we shall reap if we do not lose heart. (Galatians 6:9).*

Remember that every positive action you do for the Kingdom of God is being recorded and will be rewarded. We are living for the audience of One.

I recommend that you have a set time and stick to it. This is your personal evangelism time, and it is different from Church evangelism. You could go with your spouse, or evangelism partner or groups of friends.

Practical

Prayerfully set evangelism goals that are SMART. Specific, Measurable, Achievable, Realistic and Time-bound. If you aim at nothing, you will definitely get nothing.

Set big bold God given goals. For example, in the years 2020 to 2021, we were stirred by the Lord to share the gospel with all the people in our local area. The population was about 12,000 and 5,000 homes. We mapped the streets in the area and systematically dropped gospel tracts in every home we could access. It took about 6 months to complete., but it was done.

Break down the goals into manageable chunks. Be specific in your prayers. Envision God moving through you. We are partners with the Lord.

Monitor your evangelism goals, be accountable to your accountability partner.

In conclusion, the enemy uses deception and ignorance to present the fake, sinful life as the real deal. For example, Lion tamers in the circus use distraction (a 3 or 4 legged stools) to confuse and control the wild animals. Likewise, the enemy uses entertainment, money, fleshly desires, pride, self-achievement, self-righteousness, religion distract people from responding to Jesus.

Jesus said I am the REAL DEAL. *Jesus said to him, "I am the way, the truth, and the life. No one comes to the Father except through Me. (John 14:6). The thief does not come except to steal, and to kill, and to destroy. I have come that they may have life, and that they may have it more abundantly. (John 10:10).*

The enemy came to steal lives. To steal means to deprive someone of something that is rightfully theirs. The enemy steals people's peace, joy, fulfilment and access to a right relationship with God. The enemy paints a picture of God that is far removed and angry with them. Jesus said, no, the Kingdom of God is within you and easily accessible to you.

The enemy came to kill. To kill means to terminate, put to an end. For example, in 2021, over 200,000 abortions were recorded in the UK[1]. What about teenage murders, millions of lives terminated by war, genocide, destinies, and families terminated by drugs. Jesus said NO, I have come to give life, hope, peace, inject you with real life, God's life, the fulfilling life that derives satisfaction in God, not in things, people, money or worldly pleasures.

The enemy came to destroy lives. To destroy means to completely ruin or spoil and make irreversible damage. The enemy's mission is to ultimately get people to hell where they are ruined eternally. Jesus came and said NO, I have come so that people can be saved completely and spend eternity with me.

Will you join King Jesus in this noble task?

Reflections and Prayer points

1. Lord, help me to understand the value of a soul to you.
2. Lord, open my eyes to opportunities around me to share the good news.
3. Lord, help me to be an effective soul winner.

---

[1] Abortion statistics, England and Wales: 2021 - GOV.UK (www.gov.uk)

Chapter 10: Eternal Life

Eternal Life is one of the most used phrases in Church. If you ask the average person on the street, to explain what eternal life is, people usually say "living forever", "going to heaven" etc. The response in the Church is similar and may include phrases, like "living forever in heaven with Jesus", "having your sins forgiven and going to heaven" etc. Whilst eternal life includes the very important part of having our sins forgiven and living forever with Jesus in heaven, it is much more than that and we will be exploring that in the chapter.

What is Eternal Life?

To understand what eternal life is, it is important that we get the definition straight from our Lord Jesus, the author of eternal life. In John 17:3, Jesus explained what eternal life is. *And this is eternal life, that they may know You, the only true God, and Jesus Christ whom You have sent.* So, eternal life according to Jesus is knowing God in an intimate way. This is not an intellectual (head knowledge) but a heart-to-heart knowledge of God. There are wonderful 'by products' if I may use the phrase of eternal life, like forgiveness of our sins, having guilt and condemnation removed, the fear of death destroyed, and we live forever in heaven with Jesus when He returns or when we go to be with Him.

It was just that sin was a barrier between God and human beings and we could not relate with God as God intended. We owed the debt of sin to God that we could not repay, so God Himself became man (Jesus Christ) to pay the penalty for our sins and restore us back to a right relationship with God. Not only that, He gave us His Spirit (The Holy Spirit) to live with us and in us. The Holy Spirit is here to empower, guide, comfort, correct and reveal God to us as we grow in our relationship with Him.

In John 3:16, the Bible says *"For God so loved the world that He gave His only begotten Son, that whoever believes in Him should not perish but have everlasting life"*. You will notice that Jesus said, "have eternal life". That means that eternal life is something that you possess, and you will know whether you possess it or not. Eternal life is not a place (in this case heaven) but having eternal life here on earth will ultimately take you to heaven and live forever with Jesus there.

In fact, the phrase 'have or has eternal life' occurs several times in the Bible (Matthew 19:16, John 3:15, John 3:16, John 3:36, John 5:39, John 6:54 and 1 John 5:13). There are obviously other references in the Bible to eternal life, the point being made here is that eternal life is a spiritual tangible possession you have here on earth. We receive eternal life here on earth through repenting of our sins and summitting the whole of our lives to Jesus as our Lord and Saviour. Then we receive forgiveness of sin and the gift of eternal life.

The Implication of Eternal Life
We have the very life of God in us. We are partakers of the divine nature.

[3] According as his divine power hath given unto us all things that pertain unto life and godliness, through the knowledge of him that hath called us to glory and virtue. [4] Whereby are given unto us exceeding great and precious promises: that by these ye might be partakers of the divine nature, having escaped the corruption that is in the world through lust. (2Peter 1:3-4).

By the virtue of salvation (having eternal life imparted into our spirits), we now have access to all things relating to this life and godliness. The knowledge of God, the intimate knowledge of God that comes through fellowship, communing, obedience, reading, studying, mediating on the Word of God will position us to better access 'all things that pertain to life and godliness'.

In addition, God has given us exceeding great and precious promises. These are all accessible through the Word of God and by the illumination of the Holy Spirit. Instead of asking God to bless us, we should ask God to open the eyes of our hearts to the blessings He has already provided and help us to access them.

God has given these promises so that we can be participants in the divine nature here on earth. We are ambassadors of Christ, citizens of heaven, members of the family of God. No believer is inferior to another believer. It is the purpose of God that all His children live to their full Kingdom potential. Our calling is to be participants, not spectators of the divine nature. God's divine nature is in every believer, and He expects us to manifest it. The world is also waiting for the manifestation of the sons of God (Romans 8:26). Embrace the divine nature the Father has given you.

14 For this reason I bow my knees to the Father of our Lord Jesus Christ, 15 from whom the whole family in heaven and earth is named, (Ephesians 3:14-15). Apostle Paul expressed heartfelt appreciation for his redemption, to the extent that he bowed his knees in gratitude to our Heavenly Father. Likewise, we need to develop an attitude of gratitude for our salvation and the gift of eternal life.

As we go through the daily grinds of life, if we do not train our hearts to regularly reflect on the so great a salvation we have, our hearts could grow cold towards God. At the very least, your relationship with God becomes a drag. You are just going through the motions. Someone described as being saved and stuck. Having an attitude of gratitude also helps us to keep our problems in perspective, in the light of eternity. Apostle Paul described his problems as 'light afflictions' (2 Corinthans.4:17). That was an understatement. Apostle Paul was stoned, imprisoned, beaten, slandered, taken advantage of, experienced disappointments, forsaken and so on. But he was so eternity and heaven focussed, that the challenges of this this life, paled into insignificance. We can also be so focussed on God, His mission for our lives that our present problems and challenges though real, are put in proper perspective. We are not denying the challenges, but we should not allow problems to dominate and direct our lives.

[16] that He would grant you, according to the riches of His glory, to be strengthened with might through His Spirit in the inner man, (Ephesians 3:16). Paul prayed for the Church in Ephesus that they would be strengthened with divine capacity by the Holy Spirit in their inner man. The inner man is the recreated human spirit (the born-again spirit). That is the part of you that is a new creation according to 2Corinthians 5:17. In other words, God wants to and is willing to strengthen you with His Power through the Holy Spirit. He is not leaving you alone to figure out the Christian life on your own. The Holy Spirit is right there with you and in you to increase your capacity to live a successful Christian life. No wonder, Jesus said 'I have come that they might have life and have it more abundantly' (John 10:10b).

[17] that Christ may dwell in your hearts through faith; that you, being rooted and grounded in love, [18] may be able to comprehend with all the saints what is the width and length and depth and height [19] to know the love of Christ which passes knowledge; that you may be filled with all the fullness of God. (Ephesians 3:17-19). Paul further prayed for the Church in Ephesus to be rooted in the love of Christ. He also prayed that they would receive revelational knowledge of the love of Christ in their hearts. That they would understand the scale, scope, range and unlimited dimension of the love of Christ. To the extent that they are filled with all the fullness of God. Think about that, God wants you to be filled with His fullness. This fullness comes through revelation knowledge. It is a good practice to pray Ephesians 3:14-19 for yourself and others regularly with the expectation to grow in the revelation knowledge of God.

Saved for so much more!

It seems that many Christians' relationship with God is primarily needs driven. "God bless me", "give me a job", "give a house", "give me a spouse", "heal me" etc. God is more than willing to bless us and His blessings are part of our covenant relationship with Him. It is the Father's will do give us the kingdom; He is not withholding good things from us. He loves us more than we can ever love ourselves. No good thing will He withhold from those who walk uprightly. Beyond this, God wants us to seek His heart, not just His hand.

31 "Therefore do not worry, saying, 'What shall we eat?' or 'What shall we drink?' or 'What shall we wear?' 32 For after all these things the Gentiles seek. For your heavenly Father knows that you need all these things. 33 But seek first the kingdom of God and His righteousness, and all these things shall be added to you. Jesus instructed us to seek first the Kingdom and His righteousness. He did not say seek only but seek first. That means that God's Kingdom and His righteousness should be our number one priority. Then all other blessings will be added to us. When we reverse this order by seeking things first, then God's Kingdom, we risk living unfulfilled lives instead of experiencing God's abundant life.

God told Prophet Jeremiah "Before I formed you in the womb, I knew you; Before you were born, I sanctified you; I ordained you a prophet to the nations." (Jeremiah 1:5). Just as God called, ordained Prophet Jeremiah, God has saved, called, and ordained you to fulfil divine purpose. The eternal life that you now have is not just a one-way ticket to heaven and you just get by here on earth. No, you must desire, pray and pursue God purpose for your life. It could start with being faithful in the 'small' things like servicing in your local Church, small group or in your community. Then it unfolds into something bigger.

Application of Eternal Life
Persecution

10 But you have carefully followed my doctrine, manner of life, purpose, faith, longsuffering, love, perseverance, 11 persecutions, afflictions, which happened to me at Antioch, at Iconium, at Lystra, what persecutions I endured. And out of them all the Lord delivered me. 12 Yes, and all who desire to live godly in Christ Jesus will suffer persecution. (2 Timothy 3:10-12). Persecution is suffering cruel and unfair treatment because of your faith in Jesus Christ. Depending on where you live in the world, persecution may vary in form, from implicit poking of fun, sarcasm, mockery, insults to physical assaults, imprisonment and death.

Persecution is one thing that you cannot pray away. If you are living a godly live which aligns with the Bible, you will suffer persecution at some point. This is because the Christian culture is at its core is counterculture to the world's culture. You are in this world, but not of this world. Whilst you don't actively seek persecution, persecution will find you in some shape or form as you live for Jesus. If Jesus was persecuted, and the servant is not greater than the master, then you will also be persecuted. But be encouraged, Jesus is always with you, and He has given you the Holy Spirit, the Comforter to always be with you and in you to always strengthen and comfort you including times of trial of faith.

Resist the devil!

"Therefore, submit to God. Resist the devil and he will flee from you". (James 4:6-7). Spiritual passivity is one of the banes of modern Christianity. Yet, God has not called us to be passive, but proactive in taking a stand against the devil, his cohorts and anything in your life that does not line up with God's Word. Jesus has given you authority over all the powers of the enemy, and nothing shall harm you (Luke 10:19). Are you aware you have

authority over all the powers of the wicked one? It is not good enough to know that you have something, you must use it effectively so that it can be beneficial to you and others. Likewise, you must use the authority that Almighty God has invested in you to wade off all the attacks of the enemy, enjoy the benefits of eternal life and use it to advance the kingdom of God here on earth. Recommended books are 'The believers Authority' by Kenneth Hagin. 'The Wonderful Name of Jesus' and 'New Creation Realties', both by E.W. Kenyon.

Born of God to overcome the world.

"For whatever is born of God overcomes the world. And this is the victory that has overcome the world our faith". (1 John 5:4).

You are now born of God; you have the very nature of God in you. You now have the DNA (Divine Nature Attribute) of God. Part of that divine nature is the mandate to overcome the world system that is diametrically opposed to the system and culture of the Kingdom of God. Through your faith in Jesus Christ, you have the requirement to overcome the world. The victory that overcomes the world is your faith in Jesus Christ. The Bible did not say that you will not have challenges in life, but with the help of Jesus, you will overcome the challenges. *Who is he who overcomes the world, but he who believes that Jesus is the Son of God? (1 John 5:5).*

Love not the world

[15] Do not love the world or the things in the world. If anyone loves the world, the love of the Father is not in him. [16] For all that is in the world the lust of the flesh, the lust of the eyes, and the pride of life is not of the Father but is of the world. [17] And the world is passing away, and the lust of it; but he who does the will of God abides forever. (1 John 2:15-17). The world in this context means the values, culture, system, lifestyle, ideology, priorities that are opposed to God and His Word. Look at TV, movies, newspapers, magazines, social media etc. The lens through which they view

life is very opposed to what the Bible teaches. Therefore, God does not want us to get wrapped up in the world's system. *⁴ Adulterers and adulteresses! Do you not know that friendship with the world is enmity with God? Whoever therefore wants to be a friend of the world makes himself an enemy of God. ⁵ Or do you think that the Scripture says in vain, "The Spirit who dwells in us yearns jealously"? (James 4:4-5).* You will develop intimacy with God as you intentionally decouple from the world's system. That does not mean that you become a recluse and don't interact with others or become a weirdo. It means that you purposefully train your heart to view things through the lens of the God's Word and live by the standard of God's Word. Not what the world says is right, trendy, or acceptable.

Love God, Love God's Children and Love People

³⁵ Then one of them, a lawyer, asked Him a question, testing Him, and saying, ³⁶ "Teacher, which is the great commandment in the law?" ³⁷ Jesus said to him, "'You shall love the Lord your God with all your heart, with all your soul, and with all your mind." (Matthew 22:35-37). A person well versed in the Old Testament asked Jesus what the greatest commandment was. Jesus replied, love God with wholehearted and unrestrained devotion. That is deep. Love God with all your heart (your innermost being), your soul (emotions and will) and all your mind (thinking faculty, imaginations, and actions). Your love for God must not only have good intentions, but they must also be backed by corresponding actions. Your love for God must find expression in your life choices, entertainment, finances, priorities, family, friends, colleagues and your circle of influence.

Lukewarm, non-passionate Christians do not bring glory to God. Jesus rebuked the Church in Laodicean for their lukewarmness. *¹⁴ "And to the angel of the church of the Laodiceans write, 'These things says the Amen, the Faithful and True Witness, the Beginning of the creation of God: ¹⁵ "I know your works, that you are neither cold nor hot. I could wish you were cold or hot. ¹⁶ So then, because you are lukewarm, and neither cold nor hot, I will vomit you out of My mouth. (Revelation 3:14-17).* Get around Christians who love God, love the Word, love the things of God and want to impact the world with the love of God. If you are not getting this in your current Church, prayerfully look for one that will help you to fulfil your God given destiny.

⁹ And let us not grow weary while doing good, for in due season we shall reap if we do not lose heart. ¹⁰ Therefore, as we have opportunity, let us do good to all, especially to those who are of the household of faith. (Galatians 6:9-10). Fellowshipping with believers is crucial to your spiritual wellbeing and growth. There you will find fellowship, accountability, correction, instruction and dealing with imperfect fellow Christians. You may even come across hypocrites. Those who talk the talk, but do not walk the walk. Don't let this discourage you, instead pray for them and pray for yourself so that you do not become hard hearted towards them. The above scripture admonishes us to do good to all people, especially fellow believers. Afterall, we are in the same family (family of our heavenly Father), we are heading to the same destination- heaven and we share like precious faith. *To those who have obtained like precious faith with us by the righteousness of our God and Savior Jesus Christ: (2Peter 1:1).* Beautiful.

Part of the Christian calling is to love the unsaved and the 'unlovable'. Jesus challenged His audience *⁴⁶ For if you love those who love you, what reward have you? Do not even the tax collectors do the same? ⁴⁷ And if you greet your brethren only, what do you do more than others? Do not even the tax collectors do so? ⁴⁸ Therefore you shall be perfect, just as your Father in heaven is perfect.* The tax collectors were the most despised people during Jesus' time. They were regarded by the Jews as sell outs who worked for the Roman empire that occupied Israel at that time. They were also corrupt because they extracted more tax than they should and kept the difference for themselves. Jesus said that you are not doing anything extraordinary if you love those who love and agree with you or those in your socio-economic status. God has put His love in you so that you can love with His kind of love. This love does not discriminate, but does good to all regardless of their race, culture, background or socio-economic status because they are made in the image of God.

Acknowledge every good thing in you.

..."*That the sharing of your faith may become effective by the acknowledgment of every good thing which is in you in Christ Jesus". (Philemon 1:6).* You will grow in your faith in Christ as you recognise and acknowledge every good thing that Jesus has done for you and deposited in you. You may not fully understand them, but starting to intentionally acknowledge every good thing that Jesus has done for you is the way to go. What are some of these good things? You now have eternal life, you are a partaker of God's divine nature, your sins are forgiven (past, present and future), your name is written in the Book of Life in heaven, God loves you with the same quality and quantity of love with which He loves Jesus, you have been accepted in the beloved, you reign in life by one -Jesus Christ. He will never leave you nor forsake you.

Believe, speak and act

And since we have the same spirit of faith, according to what is written, "I believed and therefore I spoke," we also believe and therefore speak, (2 Corinthians 4:13). You will notice that believing comes before speaking. The main point is that your heart and mouth must be in alignment if you will consistently experience the life God has ordained for you. A lot of times, people say the right things. For example, "I am healed", "I am delivered" I am the righteousness of God in Christ" etc, but deep down they don't really believe it or mean it. The desired result may not be achieved, then faith and confession get a bad rap. To believe, the Word of God must become personal to you. This is God speaking to me. It is not just something you heard in Church, on the TV or radio that sounds interesting and might work for you. One way to develop personal conviction of God's Word is through mediation on the Word. Biblical meditation involves concentration on a Bible verse, zero in on it, speaking it to yourself over and over and seeing it being a reality in your life. This will take time. That is why we are encouraged to meditate on the Word, day and night (Joshua 1:8). When you then speak and or act on the Word based on personal conviction, the power of God's Word is released.

Prayer and Reflection

1. Are you seeking <u>first</u> God's Kingdom and righteousness? Is God's agenda your number 1 priority or your personal agenda / ambition?

Chapter 11: Renewing Your Mind

The Bible mentions that human beings are made of three parts: spirit, soul and body. *Now may the God of peace Himself sanctify you completely; and may your whole spirit, soul, and body be preserved blameless at the coming of our Lord Jesus Christ. (1 Thessalonians 5:23).* When you got saved, it was the spirit part of you became a new creation according to 2 Cor 5:17. *Therefore, if anyone is in Christ, he is a new creation; old things have passed away; behold, all things have become new.* It is through your spirit that you primarily contact and fellowship with God. *"God is Spirit, and those who worship Him must worship in spirit and truth." (John 4:24).*

After you got saved, you now need to retrain your soul and body to align with your new spiritual status. The process of doing this is called mind renewal. *[1] I beseech you therefore, brethren, by the mercies of God, that you present your bodies a living sacrifice, holy, acceptable to God, which is your reasonable service. [2] And do not be conformed to this world, but be transformed by the renewing of your mind, that you may prove what is that good and acceptable and perfect will of God. (Romans 12:1-2).* Mind renewal is an ongoing, lifelong discipline that will help you to become more like Jesus in your walk on earth.

Mind renewal is living life through the lens of the Word of God and leading of the Holy Spirit, rather than through the lens of your background, experience, preferences or opinions of the world. It is a fundamental shift in mindset on how you see God, yourself, others and the world. It involves making intentional moment by moment decisions to choose the Mind of Christ which already lives inside of you as a new creation rather than operating from your soulish mind the way you did before you were saved.

Constituents of the Mind

Your brain is the visible or tangible part of your mind. The mind is made up of your will, emotions, intellect and imagination and subconscious mind.

Your will is that part of your mind that implements decisions and needs to be decisive. Someone can have a strong will, weak will or a will that is moderate between both. Thomas one of Jesus' Apostles was not present when Jesus appeared to them after His resurrection. *The other disciples therefore said to him, "We have seen the Lord." So he said to them, "Unless I see in His hands the print of the nails, and put my finger into the print of the nails, and put my hand into His side, <u>I will not</u> believe." (John 20:25).* Notice that Thomas said I will not believe. It was his choice not to believe his companions. You need your will to believe God and His Word and it is deliberate and intentional. Now that you are saved, your will needs to be trained, disciplined, exercised, enlightened, educated and submitted to the Word of God and God's will. God will not force His will on you. You must decide to embrace it.

Your emotions are made up of your feelings, affections and passions. They could be positive (like, laughter, happiness and love) or negative (fear, anger, anxiety, depression). God created us including our emotions. The Bible mentions several places where God expressed emotions: God laughing in heaven (Psalm 2:4); Joy in heaven over a sinner that repents (Luke 15: 7) and Jesus wept (John 7:35). Emotions have a role to play in life. God wants your emotions to be sanctified and submitted to Him as all other areas of your life.

Reasoning or intellect is the part of the mind that deals with logic, solving problems, analysing situations and circumstances etc. God is an intelligent God who created intelligent beings, human beings are the crown of God's creation and God calls us to reason with Him. *[18] Come now, and let us reason together," Says the Lord, "Though your sins are like scarlet, they shall be as white as snow;*

Though they are red like crimson, they shall be as wool. [19] If you are willing and obedient, you shall eat the good of the land; [20] But if you refuse and rebel, You shall be devoured by the sword"; For the mouth of the Lord has spoken. (Isaiah 1:18-20).

Imagination is the realm of creative thinking. It is the part of your mind that operate with limitless possibilities. Your imagination just like other parts of your mind can work for or against you. By observation, people have and are still using the power of imagination to create amazing inventions in different human endeavours. Conversely, people have also used their imagination to cause havoc and misery for many. On a personal level, God wants you to harness the power of your imagination for your good and His glory. *Now to Him who is able to do exceedingly abundantly above all that we ask or think, according to the power that works in us. (Ephesians 3:20).*

The subconscious mind is the part of the mind that is on autopilot when you do things with thinking about it. For example, you use your conscious mind to learn how to ride a bicycle. Over time as you become proficient in riding the bicycle, you then do it on autopilot without consciously thinking about it. It seemingly becomes effortless. Your subconscious mind has taken over that aspect of riding a bicycle. God wants His Word and ways to become autopilot in us. Your subconscious mind also needs to be reprogrammed to summit to God and the Kingdom culture.

How to Renew Your Mind

The Word of God is the primary instrument for renewing your mind. The Word of God is alive and powerful (Hebrews 4:12). Jesus declared that His Words are spirit and life (John 6:63). The Word of God can make purify you (John 17:17), has creative ability (Hebrews 11:3) and transform your mind to reflect the mind of Christ (1 Corinthians 2:16).

You must approach the Word of God with the right attitude to experience mind renewal. The Word of God is settled in heaven *Forever, O Lord, Your word is settled in heaven. (Psalm 119:89).* You must settle it in your heart as the final authority. *16 All Scripture is given by inspiration of God, and is profitable for doctrine, for reproof, for correction, for instruction in righteousness, 17 that the man of God may be complete, thoroughly equipped for every good work (2 Timothy 3:16).*

The Word of God should form the basis of your prayers. In other words, your prayers should be based on God's Word. People sometimes pray based on how they feel, the hurt the have experienced or how desperate their situation is etc. Whilst not totally discounting these, ultimately, it is faith in God that gets answers to your prayers. *"But without faith it is impossible to please Him, for he who comes to God must believe that He is, and that He is a rewarder of those who diligently seek Him". (Hebrews 11:6).* Faith comes by the Word of God. *"So then faith comes by hearing, and hearing by the word of God". (Romans 10:17).* The more your prayers are based on God's Word in context, the more you are renewing your mind to God's Word and aligning to His will.

Praying in tongues is also a powerful way to renew your mind. *For he that speaketh in an unknown tongue speaketh not unto men, but unto God: for no man undertsandeth him; howbeit in the spirit he speaketh mysteries, (1Corinthins 14:2).* When you pray in tongues, especially for extended periods of time, you are training your mind to acknowledge and yield the reality of the spirit realm. Even though your mind cannot understand it, you are connecting directly with God and praying the will of God. *If I pray in an unknown tongue, my spirit prayeth, but my understanding is unfruitful. (1Corinthains 14;14).* When you pray in tongues you are building up yourself spiritually. It is like charging a battery that is run down. *He that speaketh in an unknown tongue edifies himself (1Corinthians 14:4).* You can also ask the Lord for interpretation when you pray in tongues: *Wherefore let him that speaketh in an unknown tongue pray that he may interpret (1Corinthians 14:13).*

Systematically read and study the Bible to understand the whole counsel of God. Just reading bits and pieces here and there will not help you grow and renew your mind. *"Be diligent to present yourself approved to God, a worker who does not need to be ashamed, rightly dividing the word of truth". (2 Timothy 2:15).* Studying involves diving deeper into the Word. You should use Bible references, Bible dictionaries and commentaries. You can also do topical or character Bible studies. Ultimately, you should ask the Holy Spirit to help you to study and understand the Word. You don't just to want to acquire intellectual understanding, but revelational knowledge of the Word.

Speaking out God's Word also helps you to renew your mind. You need to believe and speak out God's Word. When you speak, you hear it with your inner ear (internally) and outer ear (externally). *"Death and life are in the power of the tongue, and those who love it will eat its fruit". (Proverbs 18:21).* Since the Word of God is life, when you speak God's Word, you release the life of God into your life. Speaking out God's Word over yourself also involves personalising the speaking the Word. For example, you say out aloud, "I am the righteousness of God in Christ". This is based on the Bible verse from 2 Corinthians 5:21. *"For He made Him who knew no sin to be sin for us, that we might become the righteousness of God in Him".*

Many Christians are saved, sanctified and satisfied. Even though, deep down within then, they yearn for more. The usual and the normal seems safe. However, to experience a significant positive change, you must have a holy dissatisfaction with status quo. People who yearn for a change but do nothing about it are engaged in wishful thinking. There are lots of examples in the Bible of people who broke free from the status quo. Hannah, the mother of Prophet Samuel was dissatisfied with her childlessness and taunting from her adversary. She prayed to God with a holy desperation and got her breakthrough. (1 Samuel 1:1-19).

Before salvation, you developed thoughts, values, philosophies which may not necessarily be based on the Word of God. You are a product of your upbringing, environment, culture, education and other influences in your live. Now that you are saved, you need to deliberately change your mindset from the worldly viewpoint a Bible based viewpoint. Your thoughts imaginations and attitudes now need to be filtered with the Word of God. This is what the Bible refers to as pulling down strongholds and casting down imaginations *3 For though we walk in the flesh, we do not war according to the flesh. 4 For the weapons of our warfare are not carnal but mighty in God for pulling down strongholds, 5 casting down arguments and every high thing that exalts itself against the knowledge of God, bringing every thought into captivity to the obedience of Christ, 6 and being ready to punish all disobedience when your obedience is fulfilled.*

Notice that the Bible did not say that God will do this for you. It is your responsibility to reject thoughts, ideologies that are not aligned to the Word of God and deliberately, constantly embrace those that are aligned with the Word of God. This will involve being intentional in terms of what you watch, read, listen and the people you hang around with virtually and physically. *He who walks with wise men will be wise, but the companion of fools will be destroyed. (Proverbs 13:20).*

Deliberately mediating on God's Word is vital in renewing your mind. Biblical mediation is different from the way the world practices mediation which is based on Eastern religion practices of 'emptying the mind'. Biblical mediation involves focussing, thinking, muttering, quietly repeating God's Word to yourself. We live in a 24/7 connected world with information being constantly generated and distributed. You need to practice the act of shutting off distractions to meditate on God's Word. *This Book of the Law shall not depart from your mouth, but you shall meditate in it day and night, that you may observe to do according to all that is written in it. For then you will make your way prosperous, and then you will have good success. (Joshua 1:8).*

Fasting is the discipline of denying yourself food, pleasures and other distractions to focus on God. It usually involves taking time to read and study the Bible, pray, meditate and wait on the Lord to speak to you. The physical benefits of fasting are well documented. Beyond this, fasting is a way of crucifying the flesh and bringing it to submit to the God's Word. Regular fasting helps your flesh (body and unrenewed mind) to become better 'tuned' and submissive to God's Word and the Holy Spirit. You are therefore in a better position to release the power of God in you. Fasting also trains your flesh and renew your mind to reality of the spiritual realm and helps you to better connect with God.

Intentionally developing a positive attitude and mindset based on the promises of God's Word helps to renew your mind. Regardless of your natural inclination you can develop a positive mindset based on God's Word. "For as he thinketh in his heart, so is he". (Proverbs 23:7a) You form your thoughts, then your thoughts form you. You can choose what you think. *"Finally, brethren, whatsoever things are true, whatsoever things are honest, whatsoever things are just, whatsoever things are pure, whatsoever things are lovely, whatsoever things are of good report; if there be any virtue, and if there be any praise, think on these things." (Philippians 4:8)* Everything begins from the heart. The heart of the matter is the matter of the heart. "Keep your heart with all diligence, for out of it springs the issues of life". (Proverbs 4:23).

Hindrances to Renewing Your Mind

Lack of focus will hinder you from you renewing your mind. There are so many distractions in our 24/7 connected world. These range from social media, phones, streaming services, friends, acquaintances, entertainment, leisure and gastronomic experiences just to name a few. These could easily derail you from giving mind renewal the focussed attention it requires. Lack of focus could also come from being busy and not prioritising activities in your life. There was an account in the Bible of a man given one task to secure a prisoner. The prisoner escaped because the man was "busy here and there" (1 Kings 20:40). He failed in that single task.

In the Parable of the Sower (Mark 4:1-8) our Lord Jesus spoke about a farmer scattering seed on different types of soils. The seed represents the Word of God and the soils represent the different types of hearts. One of the soils had weeds and thorns which prevented the seed sowed from producing fruitfully. Jesus referred to this as the "cares of the world and the deceitfulness of riches" chocking the Word. If you do not give priority to your relationship with God including studying, obeying and living by God's Word, personal prayer, evangelism and fellowshipping with other believers, you will not consistently experience the abundant life Jesus promised (John 10:10). God still loves you, but your experience of Him will be limited.

Being inconsistent in mind renewal will hinder you from reaping its full benefits. The devil is working 24/7 to ensure that your mind is unrenewed and it becomes more unrenewed. It is therefore your responsibility to take appropriate actions to renew your mind and keep it being renewed. Mind renewal is like physical exercise, if you are exercising, you will reap the benefits. If you stop physical exercise, over time it will become evident. If you stop taking actions to renew your mind, the world system will step in to unrenew your mind. Mind renewal is a lifelong discipline. You need to incorporate mind renewal exercises into your daily routine, just like you do physical exercise.

Benefits of Renewing Your Mind

Various studies have linked mental health with physical health[2] and vice-versa. Renewing your mind to God's Word will improve your mental, emotional health and physical health. *[20] My son, give attention to my words; Incline your ear to my sayings. [21] Do not let them depart from your eyes; Keep them in the midst of your heart; [22] For they are life to those who find them, And health to all their flesh. (Proverbs 4:20-22).*

Renewing your mind to the Word of God will help you live a godly and successful life. *This Book of the Law shall not depart from your mouth, but you shall meditate in it day and night, that you may observe to do according to all that is written in it. For then you will make your way prosperous, and then you will have good success. (Joshua 1:8).*

Renewing your mind will help you to identify and pursue God's will for your life and fulfil divine purpose. *[1] I beseech you brethren, by the mercies of God, that you present your bodies a living sacrifice, holy, acceptable unto God which is your reasonable service. [2] And be not conformed to this world: but be transformed by the renewing of your mind, that you may prove what is that good, and acceptable and perfect, will of God (Romans 12:1-2).*

Renewing your mind will help you to crucify the flesh, yield to God and live a holy life. *[22] that you put off concerning the former conversation the old man, which is corrupt according to the deceitful lusts; [23] and be renewed in the spirit of your mind; [24] and that you put on the new man, which is created after God is created in righteousness and true holiness (Ephesian 4:22-24).*

---

[2] Mental health | The King's Fund (kingsfund.org.uk)

Renewing your mind will set you free from legalism and traditions of men which nullifies the Word of God from having its full impact in your life. *"... ¹³ making the Word of God of no effect through your tradition, which ye have delivered: and many such like things do ye". (Mark 7:13)*

APPENDIX I

ACKNOWLEDGMENTS

SO many people play different roles in my life that it would be impossible to acknowledge them all by name. It goes without saying to mention my parents: My Dad, late Pa M.T. Ojo who lived out the amongst others the virtues of faithfulness and integrity. My Mum, Ma Y.O. Ojo an embodiment of strength, resilience and diligence.

Great indebtedness to Dr Cosmas Ilechukwu, the General Overseer of Charismatic Renewal Ministries (CRM), his wife Dr Adeola Ilechukwu and the CRM General Core Group.

I will also mention the Core Group and leadership of CRM in the UK.

Finally, the entire members of CRM Agape House, London including Pastor Goodness-Amao, his wife Cecilia and family.

APPENDIX II

ABOUT AUTHOR

Adeniyi Ojo is the National Administrator for Charismatic Renewal Ministries (CRM) in the United Kingdom. He is also in the leadership team of CRM Agape House, London.

He is a graduate of Obafemi Awolowo University, Ile-Ife, Nigeria and he has a master's degree in communications and Radio Engineering from King's College, London.

He is teacher of God's Word, an avid reader and has a great passion for orderliness and personal development. He is also interested in working across racial and cultural boundaries to advance the Kingdom of God.

He is married to Toun and they are blessed with four children. When he is not working, he enjoys sports (mainly watching highlights) and having a good laugh with family and friends.

APPENDIX III

Brief History of Charismatic Renewal Ministries

CRM is the work of God and it began in the heart of students who were members of "God is Love Community" a Catholic Charismatic Renewal Movement Group at the University of Ife (now Obafemi Awolowo University).

On the prophetic level, God has been speaking to born again Roman Catholics in various ways and at different times and occasions of his intension to gather unto him a people of praise within the Catholic fold. This burden lead to the formation of a prayer cell in November 1979, which met every Saturday to pray and fast and fast for a new move of God among Roman Catholics. In answer to this Prayers God spoke on the 18th of February 1980, a prophecy that soon became the Vision of CRM.

The Prophecy reads:

"Start preparing the people for the great harvest in the Catholic Church. The harvest is ripe at now, but the labourers are few, I don't want men who are prepared but not faithful. I want men with faithful and obedient hearts. This is what I mean by you keeping my Church, feed my flock, you have to make them understand what it means it means to have authority. You are my Children, I the Lord of Host I have begotten thee. I am your Father, you are my Children. I have called you all for the Glory of my name. I want you to show the devil that you are my Children, my Own Children, the Children of the Most High God, Alpha and Omega, I am the Lord.

You have to love one another all of you, because love covered a multitude of sins. It is when you have love for another you will agree as one as the apostles did and then you shall do great and mighty things in my name. I want you all to prepare for the great battle. The devil knows and he is planning for you all. I want you all to learn to wait for me. I don't mean going on a fast but waiting to hear me speak to you.

Ask me if you are not sure of what to do, I will explain to you. You are my Children, why do you fear to talk to me? Did I not make all things for the glory of my name? You had better learn to speak, you have to speak, you just have to talk, and then I will know you are really sincere.

Take not into account what the enemy may be planning to do, for I am greater than he, I will be with you always to perform what I want you to do for the glory of my name. My glory I never shall give to any other for I am the Lord.

My own dear Children, I will always lead you on. Listen to my voice for the sheep knows the voice of the master. Learn to know when I want to speak to you and listen, listen attentively for it is for your own good. I love you all. I guard over you all jealously for you are mine, my very own".

These words of prophecy became the thrust of the National Catholic Charismatic Students, the first national expression of the work of the Ministry. Many other events took place in the mid-eighties that further substance to the vision as well as the need for the CRM to stand out distinctly with its unique identity and mission.

Today, there are over 700 CRM Churches worldwide and the work has blossomed in virtually every state in Nigeria. Outside Nigeria, CRM exist in at least 18 countries including: United Kingdom, United States of America, Canada, South Africa, Ghana, Togo, Benin Republic, Sierra Leone, The Gambia, Liberia, Cameroon, Tanzania, Uganda, Malawi, Mozambique, Malaysia, Qatar and Kuwait. CRM will reach anywhere Roman Catholics are found. The zeal of the Lord will do it.

Apples of Gold- Adeniyi OJO

Apples of Gold- Adeniyi OJO